Solanus Casey

Solanus Casey

The Story of
Father Solanus
Revised
By Catherine M. Odell

Our Sunday Visitor Publishing Division
Our Sunday Visitor, Inc.
Huntington, IN 46750

Our Sunday Visitor Publishing Division
Our Sunday Visitor, Inc.
200 Noll Plaza
Huntington, IN 46750

ISBN: 978-1-59276-181-4 (Inventory No. T232)
LCCN: 2007927217
Cover design by Monica Haneline
Cover photo by James E. Jeruzal (Huntington, IN), c. 1952
Interior design by Sherri L. Hoffman

PRINTED IN THE UNITED STATES OF AMERICA

To my wonderful mother,
Marcella Rose Anthony (1911–2005).
Like Fr. Solanus,
she showed those around her the joy and holiness
of being thankful.

Statue of Fr. Solanus outside the Solanus Casey Center, Detroit.

CONTENTS

INTRODUCTION

SEVERAL DAYS AFTER the death of Fr. Solanus Casey, O.F.M. Cap. in Detroit, Michigan, on July 31, 1957, his Capuchin brothers went to his small room at St. Bonaventure's Friary to collect his things. What they discovered was after eighty–six years of life, including sixty years as a religious, he had very little which could be called "personal effects."

Altogether, the brothers found a black-brimmed winter hat; a brown skull cap; some family photos and letters; a trunk; some books; a pair of wire-rimmed glasses; a pair of shoes; a winter overcoat; a second pair of sandals; some underclothes and nightshirts; a breviary; a violin with bow; several pictures of the Blessed Virgin; a rosary; two worn habits; and the red stole he used each Wednesday at the 3:00 P.M. healing service.

The collection was a poor man's holdings, but a much larger legacy of the man did, in fact, exist. It was the kind that couldn't be counted or evaluated in terms of dollars and cents.

"Some years ago I was in utter despair and just wanted to die," confessed a tearful woman at the Capuchin's wake. "I spoke to him and began to live again."

"Fifteen years ago, my son was dying of polio," a parent reported. "Fr. Solanus blessed him, and today he is in the best of health."

There were hundreds — even thousands — of such stories. They all had a common theme: Fr. Solanus had prayed, and things were never the same again. Many times, things changed for the better. People with cancer, paralysis, blindness, emotional illness, and tumors were among those who claimed healings through this priest. Others realized that Solanus was preparing them to accept death, the loss of a loved one, or continued suffering. But no matter the outcome, all felt blessed.

Fr. Solanus was ordained a simplex priest in 1904; in this capacity, he was denied the faculties to hear confessions or to give doctrinal sermons. Instead, this priest was given the job of friary porter, or doorkeeper; his job was to answer the door and take messages. Gradually, however, friary visitors found something spiritually magnetic about the kind, bearded priest. They began to tell him of their problems and their hopes. He reminded them of the goodness of God. He promised to pray for their needs and did so, even into the loneliest hours of the night.

Into this humble vessel, this doorkeeper, great spiritual gifts began to be poured. When Fr. Solanus prayed for others, his prayers were answered with unexplainable frequency. He was able to foresee future events and often shared his visions with others. In today's light, it seems evident that Fr. Solanus had the gifts of miracles, prophecy, healing, discernment, and other gifts of the Spirit described by St. Paul in 1 Corinthians 12. Fr. Solanus also had mighty gifts of faith, hope, and love that overflowed into all that he said and did.

His was a life that changed others, often after no more than a momentary meeting. His closeness to the Lord was so apparent that people of all ages, creeds, economic backgrounds, and cultures were drawn to him. An investigation of his cause for beatification and canonization is currently under way. As a result, he may one day be named as the first native-born American male canonized as a saint. Fr. Solanus himself would probably have blushed at the prospect. Throughout his life, he constantly asked his friends to pray for his own conversion and salvation.

Fr. Solanus Casey is an awesome and yet accessible model for our modern times. His virtues and story "translate" especially well for today's American Christians. The son of Irish immigrants, he was a Midwesterner from a big family. He could shoot a fair game of pool and loved baseball and hot dogs with onions. He was also a pilgrim in modern times and knew all about telephones, TVs, the Cold War, and consumerism. The special blessing of Fr. Solanus to American Catholics and all Christians is that he showed others that a life-giving faith and love of God could be so simple yet so powerful.

In 1976, Cardinal John Dearden, then Archbishop of Detroit, officially initiated the diocesan investigation into the heroic virtues of Fr. Solanus (Bernard) Casey, O.F.M. Cap. Since then, those who knew Solanus and those who have learned about him have been patiently praying and waiting for the day when they can freely call him "St. Solanus."

In Detroit, an impressive Solanus Casey Center, built in 2002, has become a pilgrimage site that annually draws 150,000 visitors from around the world. Pilgrims learn not only about the life of Solanus Casey but also about other saintly Christians who, like the doorkeeper, boldly lived the Christian Beatitudes and the works of mercy.

Are beatification and canonization imminent for this American Capuchin priest, the son of Irish immigrants? Br. Leo Wollenweber, O.F.M. Cap., Vice Postulator for the Solanus Cause since 1974, is a naturally hopeful man. There are plenty of reasons to believe that that great day is not too far away.

"Don't worry. God's in charge," one can almost hear Solanus Casey playfully reproaching his impatient supporters. "God knows the best way to get things done."

One day, during the Detroit days of Fr. Solanus, a small boy with a cast on his arm sat in the front waiting room of St. Bonaventure's Friary. After dozens of others moved ahead to ask the bearded Capuchin for a blessing, the boy finally moved to the porter's desk with his mother. He had heard of the wonderful healings accomplished through this priest's prayers. Suddenly, to the mother's surprise, the boy began to tug anxiously at the cast encasing his arm.

The friar with the warm blue eyes and smile leaned over the desk to speak to the boy. He knew what the child was thinking. "God's blessing goes right on through," Fr. Solanus reassured the boy. With that, he blessed the youngster's arm — cast and all — and then, the mother. The boy's face lit up with understanding and peace. He smiled back at Fr. Solanus and took him at his word.

CATHERINE M. ODELL
JULY 1, 2006

FOREWORD

WHEN I WAS ASKED TO PROVIDE a foreword for the new edition of *Solanus Casey: The Story of Father Solanus Revised*, I was both joyful and intimidated. I had the immense blessing of living with Fr. Solanus for almost a year when I was a novice at St. Felix Friary in Huntington, Indiana, in 1951. From the first day I met him, it was clear that he was a saint of God and a true mystic. Even at the age of eighteen, I was interested in such people.

When I was a teenager, I prayed often that I would know someone who would become a saint of the Church. Strangely, I have known five or six people who are likely candidates for canonization. One of them is already beatified — the great and holy Blessed Mother Teresa of Calcutta. I eventually became the postulator of the cause for the beatification of the servant of God, Terence Cardinal Cooke of New York, himself a very gentle and holy man. But the first candidate for sainthood I knew was Fr. Solanus.

To this day, having known a few such great people, I still think that Fr. Solanus was the saintliest person I ever knew. I watched him closely and, as it is reported in this book, I saw him late one night in ecstasy before the Blessed Sacrament. What struck me about him was not simply his miracles or the tremendous esteem people had for him, but his absolute, pure giving of self.

You will notice that I do not call him a "personality." Personalities are the masks we wear between our inner persons and the world around us. It is my impression that with Fr. Solanus, the mask of personality had almost entirely disappeared. With both Mother Teresa and Fr. Solanus, you were dealing with persons as they came from the hand of God.

The privilege of knowing Fr. Solanus was both fascinating and intimidating to me as a novice. Others around me related to him more as equals in the community. It is also known that some clergy were hostile to him — or, worse, amused by him.

Here was a man who had given himself completely, absolutely, and consistently to God. He wanted and needed nothing else. He wanted only to serve and give and pray. The image of this holy man kneeling for hours in the chapel late at night, even at an advanced age, is burned into my memory.

It is said that the saints are given to us so that we can imitate them. It would be impossible to imitate someone who cured the sick and foretold the future in the most inconspicuous way possible. It would also be very difficult to imitate someone who literally prayed all the time and accepted humiliations with a gentle sense of humor.

But the saints are not only to be imitated. They are to be implored. I hope and pray that very shortly, the Venerable Fr. Solanus Casey will be beatified. Then, we can pray publicly to him, asking him to intercede for us before the throne of God. We can ask that he beseech God to give us the graces to follow Christ as faithfully as he did. His life was not easy. I can still see him saying a few words at Mass since, as a simplex priest, he was not allowed to preach. There was not a dry eye in the chapel as he humbly said, "If we want to rise with Christ, we have to be crucified with Him." That was the only indication that he felt that he had been treated roughly. Many people also know that Solanus suffered terribly from the physical ailments that plagued his later years.

At no other time was I aware of anything remotely resembling a complaint. He did reveal spontaneously in that sermon that he knew what it meant to be crucified. I think that now, Solanus knows — better than most of us ever will — what it means to rise with Christ and be glorified. Hopefully, we can struggle to follow along.

FR. BENEDICT J. GROESCHEL, C.F.R.
OFFICE FOR SPIRITUAL DEVELOPMENT
ARCHDIOCESE OF NEW YORK
MAY 15, 2006

ACKNOWLEDGMENTS

THIS VERSION OF FR. SOLANUS'S STORY traces its beginning to the decade of life (1946–1956) that Fr. Solanus lived out at St. Felix Friary in Huntington, Indiana, where Our Sunday Visitor, Inc., is also located. Early in 1956, he was transferred back to Detroit, where he died in 1957. When this author lived in Huntington, many years after his death, people were talking of him and telling their own stories about him. I am thankful to all those who shared their personal Solanus stories.

Great thanks are also due to the wonderful people at the Solanus Casey Center (www.solanuscenter.org) in Detroit, where efforts continue to promote the cause and story of Fr. Solanus Casey. Br. Leo Wollenweber, O.F.M. Cap., vice-postulator of the cause of beatification and canonization (www.solanuscasey.org) for Fr. Solanus, offered his time and wonderful Capuchin hospitality more than once.

Brother Leo's personal memories of Fr. Solanus, and his cooperation in opening the archives of Solanus material to this author, were invaluable contributions. Direct quotations from the writings of Fr. Solanus (notably in the section headed "Words and Wisdom of Father Solanus" in the latter part of this work) have been left intact — grammatical inconsistencies and all — to maintain the flavor and spirit of the Capuchin's innermost thoughts. I am very grateful, as well, to Br. Richard Merling, O.F.M. Cap., Father Solanus Guild Director in Detroit. Br. Richard was enormously helpful in providing photos — even several recently acquired photos. All of this wonderful Capuchin cooperation helps this book tell its story.

❦

CHAPTER ONE

The Caseys Homestead in America (1865–1882)

IT WAS THE TWENTY-FIFTH of November, 1870 — exactly one month before Christmas — when a newborn's cry could be heard inside the three-room log house near Oak Grove, Wisconsin, just south of Prescott. The snow-topped cabin was perched upon a bluff high above the mighty Mississippi River, the boundary at this point between Wisconsin and Minnesota. But here, twenty-five miles from St. Paul — across the river and about two hundred miles from where the Mississippi River has its origins — the river was "modest" and not quite so "mighty."

The snug Irish Catholic family at home inside the cabin had origins far from Wisconsin and Minnesota. Barney and Ellen Casey were, as historians later dubbed them, "Potato Irish" — immigrants from Ireland to America during and after the years of Ireland's Great Potato Famine of the 1840s.

Bernard and his Ellen didn't fully know the size of this migration from their native Ireland; they knew only that they'd had plenty of Irish company on the crossing boats. Historians confirmed their impressions, noting later that four million Irish had sailed across the Atlantic Ocean to America from 1845 to 1900. "Poor Ireland's done," "the country's gone forever," Irish immigrants told one another in this country.

While the Caseys were still thinking of a name for the newborn boy on this cold day in 1870, his mother, Ellen Elizabeth Murphy Casey, was resting. She herself had also been born on a wintry day — January 9, 1844.

Ellen was born in Camlough, County Armagh, in what is now Northern Ireland. The Irish cherished County Armagh for its connection with St. Patrick. In the fifth century, according to tradition, the great St. Patrick had put up a church there. Armagh, therefore, was soaked in the traditions of the Church. Ellen had carried that well-rooted love of the Faith to America as a very young child.

Ellen's father died during the potato famine that scourged Ireland from 1846 to 1849. When blight ruined the potato crop for several years in a row, the result was a nationwide disaster; on the table and as a crop, the potato was the staple for this small island nation. One-fourth of the arable land of Ireland had been planted in potatoes.

After her husband's death, Brigid Shields Murphy took her children — little Ellen, an older sister, Mary Ann, and their three brothers, Patrick, Owen, and Maurice — across the Atlantic to America around 1852. The family came first to the Boston area, where Brigid had relatives on the Shields side. But, soon thereafter, the family made its way to Portland, Maine. There, Brigid and her two older sons went to work in the textile mills.

At the time, they had few other alternatives. Like most of the Irish who came, the Murphys had almost no money left once their passage was paid for. Even with jobs, grinding twelve-hour days and six-day weeks provided little more than a subsistence income. Ellen and Mary Ann boarded with a Portland housewife in exchange for light housekeeping chores. The baby, three-year-old Maurice, was cared for by a family friend.

After almost ten years of scrimping and hard labor, Brigid had money enough to move west to the region around St. Paul, Minnesota. Patrick and Owen, young men by then, had already found work there. Mary Ann had married and moved there as well. Ellen, however, stayed behind to live and work in Biddeford, Maine. Now almost grown up, she was a petite, lovely young woman with straight facial features and deep-set blue eyes.

At a Fourth of July picnic in 1860, then sixteen-year-old Ellen met Bernard James Casey, the brother of her friend, Ellen Casey. A tall, handsome, dark-haired young man, Bernard told Ellen that he'd come from County Monoghan three years earlier, and she told him about her background in Armagh. No doubt they both laughed when they realized that County Monoghan and Armagh were neighboring counties in the north of Ireland — and yet the two of them traveled all the way to America before they met.

Young Casey had just turned twenty not too long before their meeting. Born June 10, 1840, at Castleblayney in County Monoghan, he and his sister, Ellen, had left Ireland behind for America when he was seventeen. In the Boston area, their brother Terrence was already becoming established. Once he'd settled in, Bernard learned the shoemaking trade and soon went into business with Terrence.

Apparently, Bernard and Ellen felt drawn to each other from that Fourth of July meeting. In the months that followed,

This retouched photo of Ellen and Bernard Casey, Fr. Solanus's parents, was taken around 1890. They met in the United States in 1860, after emigrating from Ireland during the Great Potato Famine.

they saw each other often. Before long, Barney proposed, and Ellen wrote to her mother in Hastings, Minnesota, about her thoughts of marriage.

But although Ellen's mother was hundreds of miles away, her authority was persuasive at any distance, and she didn't want her daughter married at so young an age. So she sent for Ellen, and Ellen traveled to Minnesota. The Casey-Murphy romance would have to be conducted via letters.

As the months went by, however, it was clear to Brigid that the relationship would survive the difficulties of courtship by letter, and she finally gave her approval to the marriage. On October 6, 1863, Ellen and Barney were married in a small church in Salem, a Boston suburb. The bridegroom was twenty-three, his bride was nineteen.

For a while, the young couple lived in Boston. The Civil War had begun two years before, and wartime demand for shoes by the Union army kept the Casey brothers busy. By the end of the war in April 1865, however, the demand fell drastically. The Northern armies disbanded and no longer ordered shoes by the hundreds.

Bernard and Ellen Casey, looking for a livelihood, began to move westward in stages. They lived in Germantown, Pennsylvania, for a few months, and then went to New Castle. There, Bernard and Terrence opened a shoe store. But the brothers quickly saw that making and selling shoes would no longer provide them with a good living, and they split up.

Terrence decided to move back east to attend law school. For the young Caseys, however, the move to farming and to the Midwest seemed inevitable. The couple already had two children to support — little Ellen, born July 8, 1864, and James, born August 14, 1865.

In 1862, Congress had passed the Homestead Act, which granted 160 acres to anyone wishing to settle on and cultivate public lands for at least five years, and variations on this "homesteading" concept were adapted in many areas. Thus, in the autumn of 1865, Barney and Ellen Casey moved into the area near Prescott, Wisconsin. A small log cabin was soon put up, as was a shelter for a pair of oxen and a cow. Barney, as a new farmer, watched with amazement as his brothers-in-law showed him how to use the steel plow to break the ground. The little family of four settled in, and the head of the house registered his claim. Crops were planted during the following spring.

Most Irish immigrants who came to America settled in urban areas in the East, since they lacked the capital to move west. And, despite the fact that the Irish had come from rural settings, American agriculture on the frontier was very different than growing potatoes, or "murphies," on their small plots in close-knit communities in Ireland. In this respect, the Caseys were unusual, but they were not alone. Pierce County apparently still had plenty of room to offer to newcomers. An 1860 county census, taken only five years before the Caseys arrived, showed that only eighty-two families, including seven Irish families, were then settled there.

Although German immigrants outnumbered the Irish in Wisconsin in census reports for 1870, the Irish constituted the second largest group of foreign-born at that time. (After 1870, Norwegians poured into the state, overtaking the Irish immigrants for a ranking behind the Germans.) On the whole, the Midwest was clearly developing a German flavor. German immigrants were settling in such numbers in the Midwest that Cincinnati, Milwaukee, and St. Louis were said to form a "German Triangle."

But even though Irish neighbors were few in number, Bernard Casey felt more at home in farming than he'd been in business in the city. He meant to make it work for himself and his growing family. Like many Wisconsin farms, Casey's land had a combination of wooded acreage and prairie land. The woods provided fuel and building materials, while the prairie was relatively easy to clear for planting.

Planting and harvest seasons passed by quickly. Wisconsin was a central part of the new "wheat boom," and the Caseys planted their share of it. New strains of wheat were developed that produced bigger yields. By the 1860s, Milwaukee was rivaling Chicago as the greatest wheat-shipping port in the world. The family was flourishing, too. Mary Ann was born to the Caseys on September 19, 1866. Maurice was born November 7, 1867, and John was born February 10, 1869. Tiny John was just old enough to toddle around the bed where the new baby was lying in Ellen's arms.

With six little Caseys on the Prescott place now, and a good harvest gathered in that year, Ellen and Barney Casey had plenty to be thankful for on this particular November twenty-fifth. They may have even heard of, and taken into account, the Thanksgiving holiday that the late President Abraham Lincoln had established in 1863 in the midst of the Civil War.

The baby exercising his lungs was their fourth boy, one who had the Casey dark hair and blue eyes. Ellen and Barney believed firmly in God and that all their children were special gifts from Him. But Bernard Casey, talking it over with his wife, must have seen this new child in a slightly different light. After three sons, he decided to give this son his own first name.

The sixth child was therefore called Bernard Francis Casey. On December 18, 1870, with Christmas in the air, the baby was baptized at St. Joseph's Church in Prescott, a few miles from the homestead. At home, the baby was called "Barney," his father's nickname.

Little Barney learned to walk in the increasingly cramped cabin. He grew used to the noise of the rolling Mississippi below the bluffs. The sound of that water was one of his earliest memories, along with the distant image of his mother hanging laundry on the lines near the house. He also might well have remembered his mother shouting news across the river to Mrs. Cotter, their neighbor.

By the age of two, little Barney may also have been paying some attention to family prayer, a nightly custom. Slowly, he was learning to recognize certain prayers, including the prayers of the Rosary. Though he would not have understood the meaning of such a prayer, little Barney even heard the older Caseys ask "for a happy death and a favorable judgment." During these evening prayers, the Casey toddlers undoubtedly moved around the table from father's to mother's lap. One can imagine the impression becoming fixed in the consciousness of the children: Prayer was talking. Adults talked a lot. Adults talked to one another and to children. Prayer was simply talking to an unseen God.

Children living on the land in the last quarter of the nineteenth century would have had no question about the reality of unseen powers. Summer storms, winter whiteouts, blazing prairie fires, abundant harvests, the flowing river nearby — all these things were the result of great powers that could not be comprehended, though their work could be seen. And, in the Casey home, the God spoken to was regarded as a God who loved His children, just as Bernard and Ellen loved their own.

This daily routine included many intentions for prayer. Like other nineteenth-century pioneers, the Caseys were aware of their need for "daily bread." Practically, it was fashioned from the wheat and other crops they raised and harvested. But they understood that behind that "bread" was also a merciful Father, a Creator who gave growth to the wheat in the first place. Therefore, in the Casey cabin, prayers were recited for rain, for protection from ravaging insects, blights, or molds, and for dry days to harvest when the crops were ready. They also prayed to be spared from prairie fires and even prayed for the protection of livestock — chickens, cows, the team of oxen, horses, and pigs. The Caseys never really finished praying, as their needs were many.

Living in western Wisconsin in those days wasn't easy. Cabins like the one the Caseys were living in were, literally, rough. Logs were unhewn, chinked in between with mud. The cabins were roofed with shakes and floored with rough planks. Furniture was also scanty and crude.

By 1873, Bernard Casey Sr. had begun to set his heart on a larger place when good harvests for several years gave him the chance to save some money. But the main reason he craved more space was that his family was still growing. Since the birth of little Barney in 1870, Patrick had been born March 22, 1872, and a new baby was due in the spring of 1874. The head of the family had discovered a more spacious place for sale not far from his Prescott farm. Before the end of 1873, he bought it and moved his clan and all their belongings to a new homestead in Trimbelle Township, just a bit to the east.

With the family's move to the new property, three-year-old Barney Junior's world naturally expanded. The new Trimbelle homestead was close to a river of the same name which flowed into the Mississippi just north of Redwing, Minnesota. This farm had a bigger house and was closer to a Catholic church and school.

Little Barney would remember this second place more clearly. The house near Trimbelle, Wisconsin, he estimated later, was about twelve by thirty feet with a partial loft for sleeping. The Casey boys had the run of the loft. Their sisters, far fewer in number, bedded down on one side of a divider on the ground floor. The parents slept on the other side of the divider. Otherwise, the cabin was entirely open, with no other rooms.

Much of the country surrounding the Caseys must have seemed quite rugged. "Wild beasts and rattlesnakes seem to have been the most common cause of such anxiety," recalled Bernard Casey Jr. later. He was thinking of the worries his parents had about the safety of their children in this Wisconsin wilderness. Once, some of the boys even came face-to-face with a bear that chased them.

Some of the dangers of this area, however, had nothing to do with wild animals.

One summer Sunday during a dry spell in these homesteading mid-1870s, a prairie fire licked its way across the grasslands in the direction of the Casey homestead. Black smoke billowed toward the house and was blown ahead by the stiff winds. Prairie fires terrorized homesteaders. Houses, barns, and crops were sometimes consumed in an hour's time.

Barney Sr. and about half of his children were away at church on this particular Sunday. Since the Casey wagon would carry only about half of his large family to Mass six miles away, the other half remained home and prayed. (Thomas had been born March 11, 1874, Martha on May 5, 1875, Augustine on June 14, 1876, and Leo on March 10, 1878.) On the following Sunday, the children who had remained home the previous Sunday went with their mother while the others stayed home with their father.

As soon as she saw the fire, Ellen gathered up her children, took them out of the house, and huddled with them near a tree in one of the fields. For a while, it looked as though the house would be lost. She told young Ellen, her oldest child, to quickly hoe a firebreak in front of the house and pour holy water along it as a prayer. Though the barn was burned to the ground, the fire stopped short of the house.

Little Barney hid his face in his mother's skirts to avoid the stifling smell of the smoke. Finally, he heard her nervous breathing change. "Thank God," she murmured. One of the neighbors had run over to let the hog out of the pen adjacent to the barn. The frantic animal escaped just before the barn exploded into flames. When little Barney's father and the other children came home at about noon, it was all over. The barn was destroyed, but nothing else, including field crops, was lost.

Life on the frontier had its risks, but it also had compensations, among them a wild beauty that all the Casey children remembered long into adulthood when most of them lived in metropolitan areas.

"How rich [it was] in its variety and abundance of wild flowers and fruits and nuts and berries," wrote Barney Jr. years later, when he was a priest. "There was a pasture field for cattle as well as deer and other animals." In apparent curiosity, deer would often stop in twos and threes to watch the strange things being done by the two-legged Caseys as they went about their farming chores.

In 1878, however, a different kind of disaster hit the Caseys. The loss was much more devastating than any loss by prairie fire could have been.

Twelve-year-old Mary Ann, the second daughter, was struck with "black diphtheria." A highly contagious disease seen often in this era, diphtheria was common in the United States and western Europe. The upper respiratory system was typically affected, with a thick membrane forming up and down the air passages. Victims — usually children — ran high fevers, had sore throats, and sometimes died when the deadly membrane literally shut down their ability to breathe.

Bernard and Ellen could do little for their Mary Ann. She died after struggling for several days for breath. But the tragedy was not over. Within three days of Mary Ann's death, three-year-old Martha also died in the same way. Two children dead in less than a week! The Caseys were grief-stricken but had little time to mourn their daughters. Several of the boys, including eight-year-old Barney, also had come down with the disease.

Trying to isolate their sick children, the parents hovered over their sons, who were struggling to catch their breath. The prayers of the parents were answered. All of the boys recovered, although not without some side effects. Barney was left with injured vocal cords where the membranes had infected his throat. From then on, his voice was weak, somewhat high-pitched, and wispy, even into manhood.

Life continued in the face of losses for frontier families; in the 1880s, more than twenty percent of frontier children died before they reached five years of age. Death was usually due to primitive housing conditions and poor sanitation. And, even though their family still numbered nine children after the death of the girls — and although they believed very firmly that Mary Ann and Martha were with God — their loss was always sharp for the Caseys. But Bernard Casey Sr. did his best to house and feed his children well. Unlike many farmers, he fed his milk cows over winter and always had a large garden to provide fresh fruits and vegetables.

There was an order to the Casey life. In part, it was set by the seasons and the need to gain a living from the land. In addition, Ellen and Bernard Sr. saw to it that another order, the spiritual order, was clearly visible to their children.

By the early 1880s, the Casey family circle had expanded with more children, apparently crowding the little house to its limits. After the death of the little girls in 1878, Edward was born in July 1879, and Owen was born in January 1881. By the summer of 1882, eleven-year-old Barney was in the older half of a clan of eleven Casey children. In order, they were eighteen-year-old Ellen, seventeen-year-old Jim, fourteen-year-old Maurice (who was entering the diocesan seminary at Milwaukee), thirteen-year-old John, Barney, ten-year-old Pat, eight-year-old Tom, six-year-old Gus, four-year-old Leo, three-year-old Ed, and one-year-old Owen. With such a houseful of children, life was rich, but it also wasn't always easy on a day-to-day basis. So the Irish-born head of the Casey clan began to look for a larger frontier on which to settle his growing American enterprise — his family and his farm.

❦

CHAPTER TWO

Growing Up Well-Rooted (1882–1891)

In the summer of 1882, Bernard Casey Sr. was forty-two years old, a well-respected man who had farmed the Trimbelle place for just short of nine years. During those years, the Casey crops were bountiful. The family, too, had grown to thirteen, with eleven living children, and Ellen was expecting another baby in September.

It was that same year that Barney Sr. heard of a 345-acre spread for sale just to the north of Pierce County, in St. Croix County, and rode up to look at it. The place had a six-room clapboard house, two barns, a large icehouse, a root house, and a lake on the property. Looking it over was like entering a dream.

The Willow River, which flowed close by the good-sized farm, intrigued the Irish homesteader. Equally intriguing to Barney Casey was the fact that a railroad line ran through the property and made a stop just two miles away. This meant easy transportation, by rail or by river, for his crops. He went home to think about it, but in a short while, the deal was made. The Caseys would be moving again.

As the family prepared for their relocation, Barney's baby sister, Margaret, was born on September 23, 1882. As always, there was plenty of rejoicing over the new baby. But Margaret's birth was even more special. Since Mary Ann and Martha's deaths, until Margaret came, there was only one girl among the eleven living Casey children: the oldest child, eighteen-year-old Ellen.

After the baby was born, and the harvesting was completed, the awesome task of moving began. Household supplies, farm equipment, chickens, cattle, horses, pigs, and assorted pets had to be transported, and all with one eye to the calendar and the other on the sky; the family needed to move before a sudden snowfall could block the roads and make traveling treacherous.

Fortunately, the Caseys were tucked in at their new home before the Wisconsin winter could catch them on the open road. Bernard Casey Sr. must have smiled broadly at the blessings from heaven. He had been given such a fine farm and a healthy, happy family, including a second daughter.

Like the rest of the family, Barney Jr. was thrilled with the new spread. Though he knew he would miss the place where he had spent most of his childhood, the lake, larger fields, and sheer size of the new property better fit the scope of his twelve-year-old tastes for adventure and outdoor fun.

Except for tending to the livestock, winters meant some time off for Midwestern farmers, and the elder Casey wasted no time finding a way to turn the slack season to good purpose. He became a distributor of religious books and sold subscriptions to the *Irish Standard* and *Extension* Magazine. He would travel to St. Paul by train and return with the books, heaving them off into the snowbanks as the train passed near the Casey homestead. Knowing about what time the train passed through, several of the older Casey boys would pick up the canvas sack, heavy with books, and put it on the wagon, while their father walked back home from the Burkhardt stop, two miles away.

The Caseys enjoyed literature and music. In addition to the religious books they were allowed to read (if they didn't soil them!), they enjoyed other literature. The works of James Fenimore Cooper, especially *The Deerslayer*, were family favorites. After dinner, Barney Sr. would often push his chair back from the table after prayer was concluded, hoist the youngest child up on his lap, and read aloud.

Years later, the younger Caseys could remember hearing stories about Abraham Lincoln, the verses of Irish poet Thomas Moore, and the poems of American poet Henry Wadsworth Longfellow. In particular, the Casey children loved one long poem by the American poet John Greenleaf Whittier called "Snow-Bound."

> And ere the early bedtime came
> The white drift piled the window-frame,
> And through the glass the clothes-line posts
> Looked in like tall and sheeted ghosts . . .

So Greenleaf wrote. It was a lovely vision the Caseys saw, winter after winter.

Ellen and Bernard Casey also made sure that their American-born children were well acquainted with their Irish heritage. They passed on the stories and legends of their homeland. With a fiddle bought somewhere along the way, the head of the house would play and lead his household in singing Irish ballads.

His children quickly learned that anything he lacked in musical polish, their father compensated for with enthusiasm.

If the railroad was helping to expand literary horizons for the Caseys of St. Croix County, it was also responsible for some other very practical benefits. Before the advent of the railroads and the 1880s, all time throughout the country was local time. A clock in Milwaukee might be reading 11:05 at the same moment that a Chicago timepiece was striking 11:00. On Sunday, November 18, 1883, however, railroads throughout the United States adopted "Standard Time" to allow the trains to run "on time." People commonly went to railroad stations after that to get the exact time when the signal came over the telegraph.

Life on the Casey farm was running on its own schedule, and the patterns of religious practice and faith were unchanging. The weekly Sunday trip to Mass was now a bit farther than it was from the Trimbelle property. St. Patrick's Church at Hudson, Wisconsin, was nine miles from the Casey home. Each Sunday, at least some members of the Casey family were represented, starting out for church a full two hours before the scheduled Mass. And, as the family settled into its new home during the winter of 1882–1883, the tradition of evening prayer continued. As soon as dinner was over, Bernard Sr. called for quiet and began the prayers, including the Rosary.

At twelve, young Barney was starting to grow much faster. The bout with diphtheria had left his voice weakened and wispy, and he did not seem as strong as his brothers, but he was strong enough to love the outdoor life. Outwardly, he looked much like the other Casey boys, but there was something a bit gentler about his face and behavior. Barney played baseball aggressively, especially as a catcher, but refused to take part in the boxing matches the other Casey boys set up near the barn. His coolness to the sport mystified his brothers — this was, after all, the era of the great prizefighter John L. Sullivan! — Barney wouldn't touch the gloves that his brothers had pooled their money to buy. He gave no reasons for his distaste, and after a while, his brothers did not pressure him.

In the spring of 1883, the Caseys saw Maurice leave home to enter St. Francis Seminary in Milwaukee. At the same time, Barney eagerly traveled into Hudson to spend two weeks in preparation for his First Holy Communion. (Twelve was the customary age for First Communicants in this era.) Fr. Thomas A. Kelley, the pastor of St. Patrick's at Hudson, wanted to make sure that his communicants were well-drilled in the Faith before they received the sacrament.

Barney also "took the Pledge," agreeing to abstain from alcohol until he was twenty-one years of age. It was the custom then in Irish communities to ask young boys to make that promise before receiving First Communion. In 1840, the Fourth Provincial Council of Baltimore had recommended the establishment of "temperance" societies in all parishes to curb alcohol use, and the first statewide Wisconsin meeting of the Catholic Total Abstinence Society was held in 1871. But the enthusiasm to spread the "Pledge" was primarily an Irish interest. German Catholics didn't participate, and one German priest offered a somewhat slanted explanation for their attitude. The "Pledge" movement was a good idea for the English and Irish, he said, because "as everybody knows, they drink solely to get drunk," while Germans knew how to drink with moderation.

At the time of his First Communion, Barney had a powerful experience of the Blessed Virgin Mary. Thus, during the summer and autumn following his First Communion, he began to say his own Rosary each night, in addition to the family's recitation. He would kneel by the side of his bed and pray it quietly.

After one particularly exhausting day, Barney, aching with muscle strain and fatigue, headed toward bed with the thought that he might skip his Rosary just for that night. The Casey house was growing quiet, his brothers were already in bed, and the teenager wanted only to go to sleep. But instead, he dropped to his knees. He knelt upright, not leaning on the bed. He had seen his mother and sister Ellen pray that way as long as he could remember.

Wishing to keep the commitment to this prayer, Barney had determined to recite at least one decade of the Rosary. To his surprise, the weariness left him, and he completed the full five decades. Later that night, he dreamed that he was hanging over a huge pit with flames licking up toward him. Desperately, he looked around to see a way out. Finally, he realized that a large rosary was dangling just above his head. In the shadowy reality of dreams, he grabbed onto it and suddenly felt secure. The dream impressed the boy greatly.

This Casey farm at Hudson was much larger than the Trimbelle property had been. Barney's older brothers, Jim and John, began to share the heavier farming jobs with their father. In turn, Barney "inherited" some of the chores his older brothers had always done. Some, he relished. He was constantly devising ingenious ways to snare prairie chickens or rabbits. It was also Barney who knew right where the wild berries were and where to get the wild hops his mother needed for yeast.

When eighteen-year-old Jim got a new rifle, Barney began to shadow him and showed a keen interest in hunting. Since small game and even an occasional deer helped to feed the large Casey clan, hunting was a serious business, not merely sport. Eventually, Jim turned his rifle over more and more to Barney, who went hunting regularly with a friend, Chris Adams. He became a good shot and could typically be counted upon to bag rabbits, wild ducks, geese, or prairie chickens. With perhaps a bit less enthusiasm, he also chopped wood, weeded the garden, looked for eggs the chickens laid, and fed and watered the stock.

By the time he was fourteen, Barney was slender, strong, and wiry. He had not yet completed his elementary schooling, but that was not unusual. In agricultural communities, schooling had to follow a different sort of schedule. Fields had to be planted in the spring and crops harvested when the time was right. Children, especially the boys, were needed to help, and schooling had to be fitted around the needs of agriculture.

Until the 1880s, wheat was the principal crop for Wisconsin farmers such as Bernard Casey Sr. Within that decade, however, the soil on many farms was becoming depleted through the continual use of fields for wheat. Plagues of chinch bugs began to threaten wheat's prominence. Farm prices were falling and had been falling for some time. To add to the farmers' grief, their hard times were arriving at a time when American industry was booming and manufactured goods were more expensive.

Barney Jr. became aware that, gradually, the usual family petitions for good crops carried a tone of greater and greater need. Clearly, his father was growing increasingly concerned about the situation. During the later months of 1882, a special petition was added to the Caseys' night prayer, asking the Lord to spare the crops from total disaster.

Although these months were hard, from time to time a day would come along that provided Barney with enough excitement and fun to compensate for a heavier load of responsibilities.

On this particular day, while out in the fields with three of their younger brothers, fifteen-year-old Barney and fourteen-year-old Pat suddenly froze in their tracks. Rover, the family dog, then bounded into view, excited and bleeding from a slash down his shoulder. Barney and Pat understood what all the fuss was about when they heard a wildcat snarling from a tree not far from where they stood. Brave Rover had tangled with the cat and been cut up for his efforts.

Barney knew that there was no way to keep Rover from going at it again, and having a wildcat so close to the house and smaller children was dangerous. Without his rifle, he'd have to bag the cat some other way. "Go on up to the top of the bank and stay up there," Barney warned the other two brothers. He and Pat would handle the cat with Rover's help.

Immediately, Rover returned to snap at the cat, but the cat leapt down on him, and dog and wildcat tumbled over and over. Pat picked up a big stick with which to hit the cat, while Barney circled to within two feet of the scrapping animals and cautiously lifted a large rock. Holding it poised, he waited for Rover to move away from the cat. At just the right moment, Barney heaved the rock and hit the cat squarely on the head; it dropped dead where it was. Rover sniffed at the animal, which was suddenly still. The little boys whooped from the top of the bank and came running down to their brave brothers.

The two older Casey boys found some vines and a tree branch and strung the dead animal from it. Thinking perhaps of Natty Bumppo, the frontier woodsman they'd "met" in the books of James Fenimore Cooper, the bigger boys proudly carried the cat home. There was a bounty on wildcats, so Barney and Pat knew that the carcass would bring a needed ten dollars into family coffers. But on the way home, Barney thought of a way to get something else out of the dead cat.

A little later, a ferocious wildcat was "ready to spring" just outside the family home. Propped up just a bit, the animal looked menacing enough. Pat raced into the house and told his parents that a wildcat was crouching outside. The whole family edged just outside the door to peek. While the rest of the Caseys stood ready to rush for the door, Barney and the other boys ran from behind the trees, exposing the joke. At the end of the day, four Casey boys still hooted with delight at the terror their "dangerous" wildcat had caused.

With disappointing harvests in 1885 and 1886, Barney's studies were pushed back even farther. Along with older brothers and a sister, the boy had to look for extra work to help support the family. Barney Casey Sr. was worried but thanked the Lord for his children, who could now help save his family from desperate need. Each evening during the bleak winter of 1885, he added a prayer to the evening family prayers, asking for some profit from the crops the Caseys had worked so hard to raise. (During this time of uncertainty, Grace, the Caseys' fifteenth child, was born on March 3, 1885. The last of the Casey children, Genevieve, would be born almost three years later to the day: March 7, 1888.)

In 1886, young Barney went to Stillwater, Minnesota, a town about twenty miles from the Casey homestead, to look for work like Jim had done before him. Stillwater was a good choice, Barney's parents thought, because Fr. Maurice Murphy, Ellen's younger brother, was pastor of the parish there. Ellen, who was very close to her brother, had actually rowed up and down the St. Croix River raising pledges for the church he was trying to build! With the security of family around him, Barney could live in Stillwater with his uncle.

Barney found a job at the lumber mill in Stillwater. Lumbering, a massive enterprise in the white pine forests of Wisconsin during the last half of the nineteenth century, provided seasonal work for farmers. Some say that 400-year-old pines up to ten feet in diameter weren't uncommon, but they were cut down in the same fashion as thousands of much younger trees. Working on the catwalks built above the water in Stillwater, young Barney became a "river driver" and guided the logs floating down the St. Croix River from lumbering camps toward the mill. When the mercury plunged and the river froze over, Barney went home. The logs would remain frozen upriver in massive logjams until the spring thaw. At home, he wanted to continue to work at his schooling.

With what Barney and his brothers had made and with the proceeds from the harvest, Bernard Sr. was able to pay off debts and end the year with a surplus. By then, Maurice was also contributing toward this effort. After three years, the nineteen-year-old had left the seminary due to a condition called neurasthenia. It was a type of neurosis marked by fatigue, weakness, irritability, and localized pains. The return of Maurice from the seminary was a great disappointment to his parents, although they tried not to show it.

As he was finishing up his schooling, Barney met a girl named Rebecca Tobin, whose family lived on a neighboring farm. She was a soft-spoken girl with dark hair and dark eyes. Barney may have known her for some time, but a new feeling developed between them following a debate he participated in near his sixteenth birthday, in November 1886.

Public debates were community entertainment in those years. Barney and the district schoolmaster, a Mr. Hughes, challenged Barney's father and older brother John. The subject of the debate was: "Resolved that the intemperate consumption of alcohol has been a greater evil than war." Bernard Sr. was serving then as township treasurer and a school trustee. People liked him and his family. A crowd turned out to see the Caseys square off against one another to do battle with words and wits.

Rebecca and Barney dated for some time after that. Barney completed his schooling and decided to return to Stillwater for work, though the couple agreed to exchange letters. For a short time, Barney had a job in Stillwater as a handyman and relief guard at the state prison. The environment was a bit unsavory and rough. Nonetheless, the young man was thrilled to meet the notorious Younger brothers, members of the Jesse James gang, who were prisoners there. Before Barney left prison work, Cole Younger gave him a clothes trunk, which he treasured. Then, Barney went to look for another job.

Barney worked hard and was well liked on his jobs, yet he just couldn't seem to settle down to anything he really enjoyed. Finally, he found employment at a brick kiln in Stillwater. The other men working there, he soon discovered, were primarily of German backgrounds and had German tastes.

One day, when Barney had no lunch, one of his co-workers at the brickyard offered him an extra sandwich with Limburger cheese. Barney ate it but apparently did not think too highly of its strong flavor. "Have you ever eaten that kind of cheese before?" one of the men asked Casey later. "No, I never ate it," quipped the young Irishman, "but I've often stepped in it." The German brickmakers roared with laughter. That young Irish fellow was all right, they agreed.

But a strange and sad experience at the kiln, a few weeks later, moved Barney to think more and more about his future. While he was at work, a man fell into a deep pit filled with water. Seeing that he couldn't swim, Barney jumped in after him and soon found himself struggling with the desperate man at the bottom. Barney quickly realized that he could not calm or overpower the fellow in order to haul him to the surface. He could see that he was in danger himself because the drowning man would not release him.

For some unknown reason, Barney thought to grab for the brown scapular of Our Lady of Mt. Carmel hanging around his neck. His mother had given him the scapular a short time before. At just the moment he grabbed the scapular, he later told others, he felt himself being pulled up with the man in tow, seemingly by the scapular.

In the meantime, another man had jumped into the pit to relieve Barney. He could not get the drowning man to stop struggling, however, and finally had to let him drown in order to save himself. Barney later believed that Our Lady would have saved him and the drowning victim through some miracle with the brown scapular. Disturbed and restless again, he looked for another job. While still working at the prison, Barney had heard that future jobs might be available with the new streetcar line Stillwater was planning. When he heard about openings at last, he applied immediately. His eye was taken by the swift, sparkling contrivances. He was hired, trained, and was soon working as a part-time motorman on Stillwater's electric trolley. He wrote to his family about his new work with great satisfaction.

Stillwater's streetcar system predated similar projects in most American cities. From the 1890s on, streetcar systems could be found all over the country. They rapidly updated a city — replacing horse-drawn cars, connecting towns together through interurban lines — and were inexpensive. Young Casey was surely one of the first motormen in the country, and possibly the youngest on the job.

At some point during this period, however, Barney received an emotional setback that may have actually contributed to his restlessness at some of his jobs. Enough affection had developed between Barney and Rebecca Tobin to prompt a proposal from the young man. Marriages between seventeen- and eighteen-year-olds weren't so unusual in this era, and Barney was sure he could make a good living as a motorman in Stillwater.

In a disturbing return letter, however, Rebecca informed Barney that her mother had refused to approve the engagement. In the fall, Rebecca was to continue her studies at a boarding school in St. Paul. Whether it was clearly stated or spelled out "between the lines," Barney seemed to know that the relationship was ended.

Even worse, this letter was gleefully uncovered by three of his younger brothers some weeks after he received it, when they opened his suitcase during Barney's visit home. Just what effect this breakup with Rebecca (and the teasing that no doubt went with the letter) had on the young man isn't clear. Barney was deeply emotional, as the Caseys knew, but for the most part, he concealed his feelings. He continued to circulate generally among the young people of the area and appeared to

enjoy the give-and-take of social mixing, even if he remained
a bit remote. For a while, he seemed to be attracted to Nell
O'Brien (although Nell later married his brother John), but
after Rebecca, there was no serious girlfriend apparent in his
life again.

In mixed groups, the young man would grin, tell a few stories, and pull out his harmonica or the violin he had learned to
play. His brothers, sisters, and his friends would laugh. Years
earlier, during his first attempts at "scraping," his brothers had
insisted that he practice his fiddle in the barn. Barney's playing still wasn't good, but it was lively, and he knew the latest
tunes.

When a new motorman's position opened with a streetcar
line in Appleton, Wisconsin, 230 miles away from "home,"
Barney took it. He seemed to want to get away, to travel a little farther from the west central areas of Wisconsin that he
knew so well. The Appleton job would give him that change of
scenery.

By 1890, however, Barney wanted to move closer to his
family again. He took a job with a streetcar line in Superior,
Wisconsin, about 125 miles from the Caseys' homestead. After
jumping from job to job, Barney had more or less settled into
work as a streetcar motorman. Streetcars — although quickly
catching on from city to city — were still new enough that two
or three years of experience still gave him a sort of "seniority"
in this line of work.

The Caseys were elated to have Barney closer to home,
even if he couldn't really help with problems there. It was 1891,
and American agriculture was suffering from a widespread
depression. Drought and insects had devastated crops for several years in succession. When Barney Jr. saw that there were

The Casey clan posed for this family portrait on August 14, 1892, in Superior, Wisconsin. In front, starting from left: John, Margaret, Mrs. Casey, Genevieve, Mr. Casey, Grace, Thomas, and Maurice. In the back row, from left: Edward, Leo, Bernard (the future Fr. Solanus), James, Ellen, Patrick, Owen, and Augustine. Two other children, Mary ann and Martha, died in childhood in 1878.

plenty of jobs in Superior, he wrote to his family to tell them of the opportunities.

Barney's three older brothers, Jim, Maurice, and John, moved to Superior almost at once. The four Casey boys rented a house together, and their sister Ellen temporarily quit her teaching position to care for the house and them. Barney wrote to his parents again and urged them all to come to Superior. Finally, later that same year, the head of the family sold the Burkhardt farm to a real estate company in exchange for ten city lots in Superior. Before long, Bernard Casey Sr. moved the remaining Caseys, family belongings, and all of the livestock, north to Superior. With a new rented farm and their older sons working at good jobs in the city, the family was soon on better financial ground, so much so that Bernard and Ellen could build a ten-room house to accommodate the family.

The three little girls — Margaret, Grace, and Genevieve — were enrolled in Sacred Heart Church's parochial school, while the older Casey children began to attend high school. Even John, a year older than Barney, went back to school. Thinking of a profession as a lawyer, he took up the study of law during the evenings. Life was settled and satisfying for the Caseys. Except for Barney.

One autumn afternoon in 1891, he was at work, and his streetcar was making its usual run when, as he rounded a corner, the young motorman spotted a cluster of people on the tracks ahead of him. He hit the brakes immediately, and the streetcar screeched to a halt. Barney and his passengers poured out to see what had happened.

Lying on the tracks, in a pool of blood, was a young woman. A drunken young sailor hovered over her, cursing and clutching a knife dripping with blood. As policemen pulled away the murderer at gunpoint, others lifted the woman's lifeless body off the tracks. At almost twenty-one years of age, Barney Casey Jr. had lived most of his years on the farm among peaceable people. The dead body and the drunken words of hatred introduced him to something new, something sad and evil. The event was a shock to his psyche. Barney gathered his passengers and went back to work but, at a deeper level, the young man couldn't stop brooding about the senseless murder on his tracks.

Of the many sons of Bernard and Ellen Casey, this namesake son was one of the most introspective, and Barney agonized about the direction of his life as never before. Since the broken romance with Rebecca Tobin, he had had few goals for his future. While the family still needed financial help, Barney put concerns about his own future aside. He felt obliged to help his family. But now, the family was secure again, and old questions that had preoccupied him from time to time resurfaced.

Barney began to debate something deep in his heart. He'd done plenty of rhetorical debating in the past. This time, however, the exercise was not for fun. Ellen and Bernard Sr. weren't sure what was going on inside the handsome young man, but after a long time, Barney himself was finally sure. He went to see Fr. Edmund Sturm, the pastor of Sacred Heart Parish in Superior, to discuss the priesthood. Quietly but quickly, the young streetcar motorman was starting to move his life onto an entirely new track, and in a new direction.

CHAPTER THREE

Following a New Direction (1891–1898)

Wʜᴇɴ Bᴀʀɴᴇʏ ᴡᴇɴᴛ ᴛᴏ ᴛᴀʟᴋ with Sacred Heart Parish's Fr. Edmund Sturm, he knew only that he wanted to move toward priesthood. Beyond that, he had almost no ideas about the kind of ministry he wanted to do or the sort of seminary he should choose.

Fr. Sturm listened to the young man seated in front of him, dressed in the trim, dark uniform of a streetcar motorman. He seemed a likable fellow. Though the Caseys had only recently moved into his parish, the pastor had heard quite a bit about them. He was very impressed with the young man's parents, Ellen and Bernard Sr. Superior was also impressed with the "Casey All-Brothers Nine," a baseball team composed of the Casey brothers, for which young Barney fearlessly played catcher.

After listening to what the young fellow had to say, Fr. Sturm quietly suggested that he apply for admission to St. Francis de Sales Seminary in Milwaukee. This was the same "German seminary" where Barney's brother Maurice had been enrolled. His brother's attempt to study for the priesthood there had ended disastrously, Barney knew very well. Maurice had come home convinced that he was both a failure and a deep disappointment to his family. But Barney took Fr. Sturm's advice and made plans to follow the path Maurice had taken. He believed that this was the life God wanted for him, and that God would move him toward this goal.

Barney stood up, shook hands with his pastor, and left. The anxious, heavy feeling that had been burdening him seemed to be gone. He walked out of the rectory and made his way to the streetcar station, where he was to begin work within the hour. Later in the day, he thought to himself with a smile, he would tell his family about the new track he would be taking.

At the Casey household, Barney's news was greeted with great joy. Ellen and Bernard Sr. were almost speechless, although they had suspected that their Barney was thinking of such a move. Their son explained that he would have to enroll on the high-school level with fourteen-year-old boys. At that, fifteen-year-old Gus told Barney that he would be one semester ahead of his older brother, who would begin in the middle of the school year. But Barney wasn't disturbed by that prospect. In fact, he was eager to begin.

So in January 1892, a mere few months after the streetcar episode in Superior, Barney was back in school in cold and snowy Milwaukee. This was a whole different world, conducted in a language he didn't know. At dinner, during recreation, and in classes, young Casey found himself immersed in a German world. Barney probably didn't realize it, but St. Francis Seminary was already at the center of controversy over ethnic bias — a common concern during these decades of immigrant settlement. Long before he set foot in St. Francis, the controversy had been brewing.

The Diocese of Milwaukee was founded in 1843, and the diocesan seminary had begun to enroll young men in 1856.

Even in its first year, according to its rector, Fr. Michael Heiss, German and Irish Catholics were defensive about the seminary's direction. "Some thought that the seminary would become an institution solely for the Germans. When, however, we also accepted Irish youths, certain parties spread the suspicion that it was planned to displace the Germans gradually and to make the seminary Irish."

German worries were largely misplaced. The diocesan seminary began with a German staff and emphasis, and remained that way for some years. The seminary staff was assigned by Bishop John Henni, the first bishop of Milwaukee, who had come with strong German associations from the diocese of Cincinnati. Nonetheless, it was true that the Irish clergy — both the native-born and foreign-born — were clearly trying to gain their own foothold in the German establishment. German clerics in Wisconsin undoubtedly felt that defensiveness about Irish leadership was justified. Over half of all Catholic bishops in the United States from 1789 to 1935 were Irish, even during decades when Irish Catholics represented only seventeen percent of the Catholic population. German Catholics had a saying that expressed this fear: *Mit der Sprache ghet der Glaube* ("With language goes faith"). If they lost their right to worship in their native tongue and to teach their children that language, they feared that their children would lose the Faith as well.

When Archbishop Henni was about to retire in 1878, both American and Irish priests wrote letters aimed at discouraging the appointment of another German. They wrote to Archbishop James Gibbons of Baltimore, pointing out that ,in Wisconsin, the Archbishop of Milwaukee and the bishops of the other two dioceses, La Crosse and Green Bay, were German, as were all ecclesiastical officials. There had never been an

English-speaking priest in any of these positions. In spite of these efforts, however, Archbishop Michael Heiss, the German bishop of La Crosse, succeeded to the archbishopric in 1880, and was followed by another bishop of German background, Frederick Xavier Katzer, in 1891.

Barney Casey came to Milwaukee just about one year after the archbishop. Thus, while Archbishop Katzer struggled with Irish-German sensitivities at the chancery across town, one of his newest seminarians did battle in the classroom.

This was a German seminary, and German and Latin were required courses. It was in the academic arena that he began to understand the pains and frustrations that life can bring. Stress — and, possibly, living in the cold rooms in this five-story seminary near Lake Michigan — contributed to his frequent attacks of "quinsy sore throat."

Barney was well-liked at St. Francis. Though quite a bit older than his classmates, he did not put himself above them in any way. To help pay for his tuition, he even became the seminary barber. Since students rose at 5:30 A.M. and were required to follow a rigid daily routine, the barbering job took time away from study, and Barney struggled to fulfill all of his obligations.

Although he had to work hard at his studies, Barney also took time to skate on the big rink during the winter and to play ball during the warmer months. When he assumed the role of catcher for the first time, however, he shocked his classmates; to their horror, and despite their appeals, he refused to wear a catcher's mask. With a quiet grin, the wiry young man simply made a huge Sign of the Cross in the air where balls would be zooming in and bats would be swinging at dangerous speeds. Then, he crouched down on his haunches and proceeded to play.

This approach seemed to epitomize his particular spirituality: those who came in contact with him sensed a deep spiritual quality about him. He was extremely and deeply prayerful, they noticed. But he was very approachable, too.

Despite his busy schedule, Barney did extremely well at his studies during his first semesters. The school years of 1892, '93, and '94 passed in a blur of unceasing work, broken only by some vacation and time spent with his family back in Superior. During the 1894–1895 school year, Barney was able to raise his grades high enough to enter the "fifth class," which was actually the first year of college seminary training. During the second semester of the 1895–1896 term, however, his grades dropped seriously, and seminary officials brought the young man in to talk to him frankly. They told Barney they doubted he could handle the academic demands that further college-level seminary work would require of him.

Barney couldn't completely understand their concerns. He had earned grades in the 70s in Latin, algebra, geometry, and history, and in the 77-to-85 range in German. In vocal music, U.S. history, and natural philosophy, his marks were in the 85-to-93 range. His grades in Christian doctrine and English were also good, just as they had been during the first semester. His marks were a bit low in some areas, but he clearly was not failing, so it mystified him as to why he was being dismissed from the diocesan seminary.

Bewildered, he prepared to leave Milwaukee, believing that his journey toward the priesthood had abruptly come to a halt. But then, diocesan seminary officials assured Barney that he did, indeed, seem to have a vocation, and suggested that he might be more suited to seminary study in a religious order. So

Barney took their advice and went to visit the Capuchin seminary in Milwaukee, also called St. Francis Seminary.

Once there, however, a great heaviness began to fill the young man. The hint of austerity, the unkempt beards, and the somber setting at the Capuchin seminary depressed him, and he left the Capuchins quickly. He headed home for Superior under a cloud that his prayers did not seem to lift. At twenty-five, and after four and one-half years of work, his dreams of serving the Lord were already dissolving, seemingly for no reason.

In the months that Barney was still wondering why he'd been dismissed, an editorial appeared in the Milwaukee *Catholic Citizen*. The editorial writer noted that Wisconsin state colleges, Marquette College in Milwaukee and Sacred Heart College in Watertown, had all graduated a large number of Irish-Americans that year. But, the writer added, the graduating classes of Pio Nono College and of the diocesan seminary were composed entirely of German- and Polish-Americans. The *Catholic Citizen* challenge continued:

> What is the explanation of the situation? Is there a dearth of vocations for the priesthood among the Irish-Americans of Wisconsin? Or is there something inhospitable about the atmosphere of St. Francis? We pause for meditation.

It's likely that the editorial never came into Barney's hands. He was disturbed, but his feelings were more confused than angry. He watched as his brothers pursued their goals. Jim became a mail carrier, while Maurice became a plumber and was traveling. John managed the dairy business for Bernard Sr. while studying law. Ellen, his oldest sister and now in her early thirties, had recently married Thomas Traynor. Edward was in high school but was thinking about the seminary himself, while the younger children were still in grade school. His siblings seemed to have no lack of direction and knowledge about the paths they needed to take.

In the throes of great distress, Barney succumbed to his bothersome throat ailment throughout the summer of 1896. His mother and sister Ellen tended to him and supported him in shouldering the pain in his spirit, but summer and autumn were still a torment for him.

Two matters needed clarification in his mind: whether he had the call to the priesthood in the first place, and which religious order he was to join in order to study again for ordination. On August 23, he wrote a letter to Fr. Bonaventure Frey, provincial of the Capuchins. They had already agreed to accept him if he decided to join them. Barney wrote:

Dear Rev. Father:

I received your welcome letter of the 20th a few days ago. I would ask now what I should do with regards to books, clothes, etc., as also when your scholastic year begins. I suppose you were informed about my bill of $525.00 at St. Francis. What should I do about that before I go to join you? — supposing I could not pay cash.

Hoping to hear from you again soon I am, very Rev. Father!

Yours sincerely
Bernard F. Casey

Finally, toward the end of the year, after months of anxiety and prayer, Barney asked his mother and sister Ellen to join with him in praying a novena. He needed to have this matter of a vocation made clear. They readily agreed to his request and joined him in asking heaven for direction. Thus, the novena began.

On December 8, on the Feast of the Immaculate Conception, Barney was praying after receiving Holy Communion at his parish church, Sacred Heart, in Superior. The novena was almost over. On this day, a feast of the Blessed Virgin, he made a private vow of chastity. No matter what decision was made about religious life, he would give his total devotion to God.

Then, in the midst of his quiet prayer, he received a very distinct message in his heart. The message said, "Go to Detroit." Barney knew the meaning of that! It could only mean that he was to join the Capuchins, one of the three major branches of the Franciscan order. The Lord had been faithful and answered his prayer.

When he finally left Sacred Heart, Barney felt like a new man. His heart was filled with gratitude for the Lord's goodness. He jogged home to tell his family of his new call to the Capuchins. Then, he set about learning more about the order he was to enter.

Established in Italy as a separate branch of Franciscans in the seventeenth century, the Capuchins were named for the *capuche*, or hood, attached to their brown Franciscan robes. They were founded by Matteo da Bascio and two others in the sixteenth century. Da Bascio's little band longed to follow the Rule of St. Francis "to the letter." Theirs was to be a more strict observance and a life based on absolute poverty, such as St. Francis had lived.

The order quickly gained many members in Europe but was later diminished by plagues and political oppression. Around the time of its greatest decline in membership, in 1883, a Capuchin province was established in America, with its base in Detroit.

The two founders of the Capuchin outreach to America were Fr. Francis Haas and Fr. Bonaventure Frey. When they came, these two were not even Capuchins — they were diocesan priests from Switzerland — but they had a commitment to the Capuchin charism. The two priests had arrived in America in 1856, the year before Barney Casey Sr. arrived from Ireland. In the years that Barney Casey Sr. was founding a family and livelihood, the Capuchin founders were setting up missions in Wisconsin, Michigan, and near New York City.

The Capuchin history was impressive, but Barney Jr. contemplated it with mixed feelings. The message about going to Detroit wasn't one he'd have been likely to "invent" for himself. He had been uncomfortable at the Capuchin house he'd visited in late spring. It was quite formal and austere. The Capuchin monks wore beards in imitation of St. Francis, and this bothered Barney. Not so much because of the beards themselves — his own father had always worn a beard — but because the Capuchins left their beards untrimmed, out of respect for the Franciscan call to simplicity. The thought of that didn't appeal to Barney Jr. at all. He was aware that his abhorrence of Capuchin whiskers was a minor factor; yet there was really nothing else about the prospect of joining the Capuchins that appealed to him, either.

Regardless of all these doubts, by December 20, he was ready to "go to Detroit." Because it was so close to Christmas, his family wanted him to stay and spend the holiday with them.

They knew that it would be years before they would see him again. But Barney would not yield. It was, he insisted, time to go.

In the midst of a blinding snowstorm, he left Superior on December 20 and headed southwest for St. Paul on the 11:00 P.M. train. From St. Paul, his train then headed east, pulling along slowly through drifting snow to Milwaukee. After a brief layover there, during which Barney stayed with Capuchins for the first time, he boarded a train again. Down through Chicago and over to Michigan, his train headed for his goal — Detroit.

On Christmas Eve, the train pulled into the station in Detroit at last. Barney located a streetcar and headed for Mt. Elliott Avenue. There, at 1740 Mt. Elliott, the young man finally arrived, well after dusk. Exhausted, he refused the offer of dinner; he could see no farther than a bed at this point. Upstairs, on the second floor, he was shown to his room: a simple, stark little space with a wooden door latch. The sight of it immediately renewed his fears of this Capuchin austerity, but even those thoughts were too much for the young man. Spent with the strain of travel and a difficult decision, he pulled off his shoes and heavy coat, still wet with snow, hung up the coat, pulled a blanket up over himself, and soon fell into a very deep sleep.

Just before midnight, he awoke to the sound of hand chimes and the voices of men singing. They were singing Christmas carols in German. It was Christmas Eve! As the voices grew louder, Barney could hear other men getting out of bed and coming down the corridor to join their voices with the little group of carolers. Barney joined them, and his heart was lifted. The gloom over his decision to follow the Lady's orders and "go to Detroit" left him.

Down and around, through the darkened corridors, the carolers moved. Carrying candles, they roused the other Capuchins, who then followed them down into the chapel for Christmas Midnight Mass. It was a moving, joy-filled occasion and initiated a week or more of festivities.

Once that week passed, however, the same anxieties about his decision plagued Barney once again. The transition to the new year provided no fresh hope or renewed vision that his future here could be happy and fulfilling. Capuchins were invested with the habit very soon after entrance, and he dreaded the finality of that.

His investiture into the novitiate was set for January 14, 1897. The closer the date came, the more anxious he felt about his decision. Penning his thoughts into his small book on the Rule of St. Francis and the Constitution of the Capuchins, he referred to this day of investiture as a "day of anxiety," and its coming looked to him as "dark indeed."

On January 14, however, Barney finally slipped the heavy brown cassock over his head and pulled on the Franciscan's heavy sandals over his socks. Perhaps he pulled some new vision or a feeling of peace over his psyche at the same moment. Whatever the reason, the actual investiture seemed to settle his spirit. Those painful anxieties and second thoughts seemed to dissolve into the wide, high hallways of the friary that he would come to know very well.

From the fourteenth of January, Barney Casey was known among the Capuchins as "Frater" (or "Brother") Francis Solanus Casey. St. Francis Solano, a Spaniard, was a violin-playing Franciscan missionary in South America during the seventeenth century. Francis Solano had had a powerful gift of preaching and had taken the pains to learn so many of the local dialects that he was thought to have the gift of tongues! In July 1897, seven new men entered the novitiate program to join Frater Solanus and two other novices, Leo Steinberg and Salesius Schneweis. Life in the novitiate was rigorous but not a novelty to the young man from Superior; for four years, he had lived a very ordered life at St. Francis de Sales Minor Seminary. Because the new Frater Solanus had entered the Capuchin novitiate in January, instead of in the summer as men usually did, he was between regular groups. Fraters Leo and Salesius were six months ahead of him in the novitiate, and the seven new men were six months behind. Frater Solanus's novitiate was to be longer because the vows ending the novitiate were made only in July.

Day by day, Solanus merged his life with the schedule of the friary. It was certainly different from the life he had come to know as a conductor on a streetcar line. In that life, he had kept his pocket watch handy to double-check the time. Being at the right intersection, at precisely the right minute, was important.

By contrast, inside the monastery, men walked, talked, ate, and slept in a pattern hundreds of years old. The proximity of the twentieth century changed life here very little.

Solanus and the other friars were wrenched from sleep each day at 4:45 A.M. The youngest brother would walk up and down the halls where the friars were sleeping in their rooms — called cells — and clap two two-by-four boards together to awaken the rest of his brothers. After this harsh awakening, the friars then had fifteen minutes to wash a bit and don their brown habits and sandals before they went to the chapel.

Each friar's cell was simple and spare. That of Frater Solanus, like those of other Capuchins, was a room of about nine by twelve feet. In every cell was an iron bed with a corn husk mattress and a pillow. The pillowcases and sheets were made from mattress ticking. There was a window, but it had no curtain. A small table, a small armless chair, and two clothes pegs on the wall rounded out the "furnishings." There was no closet. Capuchin brothers could hang all the clothes they owned on those two hooks.

At 5:10 A.M., the day of prayer began with Lauds. The Litany of the Saints, private meditation, and the Angelus, said just before 6:00 A.M., prepared the friars for Mass, which began at six o'clock. At seven, breakfast was served in the refectory. It was simple — cereal or bread and coffee. It was eaten in silence. Any time remaining before 8:00 A.M. was used for spiritual reading. At eight sharp, the workday began. For the Fathers in Detroit, the workday might mean confessions, preaching missions at parishes, or officiating at funerals at Mt. Elliott Cemetery, across the street from the friary. The Capuchin priests also officiated, when needed, at parishes around the city of Detroit on weekends.

The Capuchin brothers, also in residence at the monastery, shouldered the jobs of food preparation; making, repairing, and cleaning clothes; maintaining the building and grounds; running the printing press, and performing office jobs, such as serving as doorkeepers and the like.

The novices — both the clerical novices and those headed for the brotherhood — had classes to attend during the day. The novices who hoped to be priests also had other readings to do. They had to learn to say and participate in the reading of the Liturgical Hours and also helped a great deal with liturgical services throughout the year. The novices, including Frater Solanus, could receive letters from home, but the novices were not allowed either to have visitors or to visit home during this novitiate period.

In the refectory, benches and narrow refectory tables lined the walls of the large room. Friars therefore sat on the benches with no one seated across the table from them. At noon, dinner was served during which one of the Fathers read aloud from one of the Gospels. Other readings were also taken from the life of a saint, some devotional work, or from one of the papal encyclicals. One priest would read for a while and then hand the reading on to the next. This reading during both dinner and supper emphasized that no time was to be given to aimless socializing. The rule of silence was therefore observed during the meal but was lifted for Thursday meals, Sunday meals, and feast days.

After the noonday meal, the friars spent a half hour in recreation, while the novices spent some time individually in their rooms. Still later in the afternoon — from three to five o'clock — the novices engaged in manual labor. Generally, this was outdoor work, which gave the young men some needed fresh air and an outlet for stored-up physical energy. Whether in the garden or inside the monastery in the kitchen or chapel, the novices worked under careful supervision. Back in the chapel, the whole community gathered to read the Liturgical Hours before supper. Then there was recreation time, followed by some private time and the Hours again. The day was ended at 9:30 P.M. At that point, all the friars were in bed following a full day of prayer, physical exercise, and — for the novices — classroom work and study.

If Frater Solanus was not always asleep just as his head hit the pillow during these long novitiate days, his thoughts turned to his novitiate experience and what he was learning about himself. Like the other Capuchins, he kept a private notebook and recorded his thoughts about his life at St. Bonaventure. This practice of keeping a journal, with the guidance of his novice director, enabled Solanus to experience a growing understanding of his own personality and spirit.

In his journal, it is clear that Frater Solanus was struggling to purify his motives and his heart. He began to see that he operated out of a single-minded intensity in accomplishing tasks. There was certainly no moral or spiritual fault to this tendency. But it was accompanied, he came to see, by a leaning toward perfectionism that was too rigid — a spiritual scrupulosity. Gradually, he loosened up, learning to lean more on God and less on himself.

Solanus also discovered, through his journal and almost daily conversations with his superiors, how very emotional and impetuous he was by nature. Perhaps, in the context of a large, well-disciplined Irish Catholic family, such personality traits are invariably submerged or played down, especially in boys. Few of his fellow novices recognized these traits. From what they could see, Solanus was an understanding, considerate, friendly fellow very intent on growing in holiness as a Capuchin.

As hard as he worked at his studies, he worked even harder on himself. He understood that the purpose of the novitiate was not to remake him but to take the personality and gifts already there and to develop them further for service to God and others. That was the idea behind the disciplines of the monastery. Capuchin spirituality, or Franciscan spirituality, was attempting to clear away some of the clutter of self-interest and self-indulgence that almost naturally attach to men and women who live life as though it were a right and not a gift.

During this novitiate year, the young man penned in his notebook a sort of plan of action for learning to love God. It reflected the analytical, precise side of his nature. But the five-part plan showed great spiritual maturity as well. The twenty-six-year-old counseled himself to adopt:

1. Detachment of oneself from earthly affections: singleness of purpose.
2. Meditation on the Passion of Jesus Christ.
3. Uniformity of will within the divine will.
4. Mental prayer, meditation, and contemplation.
5. Prayer: "Ask and it shall be given to you" (Matthew 7:7).

As passing years revealed, the plan was not one Solanus would outgrow. It was a good guide for a second-generation Irishman anxious to live a life of Christian spirituality, in a German order, in twentieth-century America. In fact, it was a good guide for any Christian to follow. The novitiate year increasingly showed that spiritual promise would not be the thing for Frater Solanus to worry about. Again, as it had years before, his academic performance became the concern.

By the end of 1897, Capuchin superiors had already noticed that young Casey struggled with class work. Perhaps it all related to the difficulty he still had with Latin and German. Some kind of mastery of these languages was a prerequisite for ordination within this religious order. It could also be that his problems were more general than the difficulty of coping with languages. The Capuchins watching the young man were not sure.

The superiors discussed their reservations with him, a necessary step, because in July 1898, the novitiate period would be up. By then, it would be time to either accept or reject all the novices as Capuchins. If Solanus could accept the prospect of living out his life as an unordained Capuchin — simply as a religious — there was no barrier to that. But his superiors simply weren't convinced that he could master the material necessary for a man who would be ordained as a priest.

As hard as he had worked, both at St. Francis de Sales Seminary in Milwaukee and now in Detroit, such news must have grieved Frater Solanus. He knew, too, how disappointed his parents and family would be if he could not be ordained. If he was bitter about the prospect of laboring in vain, however, he did not openly express it. Possibly he simply suffered with the news and then worked hard to apply his own guidelines to the situation — detachment, meditation on the sufferings of Christ, and conforming to the will of God.

The culmination of concern about his academic potential was a signed statement he was asked to make. He wrote it and signed it in the presence of his superiors on the day before he was to take his first vows of commitment as a Capuchin. The statement was put into the monastery record on July 20, 1898. Frater Solanus Casey wrote:

> I, Fr. Solanus Casey, declare that I joined the Order of the Capuchins in the Province of St. Joseph with the sure intention to follow thus my religious vocation. Although I would wish and should be thankful, being admitted to the ordination of a priest, considering the lack of my talents, I leave it to my superiors to judge on my faculties and to dispose of me as they think best.
>
> I therefore will lay no claim whatsoever if they should think me not worthy or not able for the priesthood and I always will humbly submit to their appointments.

Why was such an "attestation" asked of a young man who ached for ordination to the Lord's priesthood? Frater Solanus already understood very well that his superiors were not guaranteeing his ordination just because he was now professing his first vows within the order. Whatever the reason, it must have been a very difficult piece of paper to sign. Solanus believed that he had a vocation to the priesthood. With this statement, he was surrendering his own deeply felt call to the will of his superiors.

On July 21, the day after he signed the attestation, Frater Solanus made his first profession of vows along with the other novices in his class. Each man vowed and promised to "live in obedience, without property, and in chastity" (the official vow formula for Capuchin Franciscans). With such a solemn promise made, kneeling in the presence of all the other friars, each man rose as a recognized member of the Capuchin order. A critical landmark in religious life had passed.

After taking their vows, Solanus and the others in his class prepared to take the train for Milwaukee. There, at the Capuchins' St. Francis Seminary, the young men were to continue their studies for the priesthood. It was a place Barney Casey had visited in the spring of 1896, after he was asked to leave the diocesan seminary. He had not been impressed with the Capuchins or their apparent austerity on that day.

More than two years later, on an early August day in 1898, Frater Solanus settled into the friary in downtown Milwaukee. He now lived under the watchful eyes of sixty-eight-year-old Fr. Anthony Rottensteiner, who directed the training and schooling of the seminarians. He had a reputation as a rigid taskmaster in and out of the classroom. The last leg of young Casey's journey toward priesthood was beginning, but it was to be more difficult than he could have imagined.

CHAPTER FOUR

A Capuchin Vocation
(1898–1904)

It WAS HOT ON THE TRAIN from Detroit to Milwaukee, a typical July day, as Solanus and the other five novices watched the midsummer countryside pass by. The train dipped southwest from Detroit, down through the rest of Michigan, skimming the northwestern corner of Indiana, and then into Chicago. From there, the route headed north, hugging Lake Michigan all the way up to Milwaukee.

In a way, Frater Solanus mused to himself, it was the reverse of the wild, wintry ride he'd taken to Detroit eighteen months earlier. The green fields he saw now had been filled with blowing snow then.

Solanus watched the world go by and stroked the dark beard which now covered his lower face. God was directing his life, he felt very sure, and he supposed God was directing his beard, too. When he thought about it that way, a beard — and even other difficulties — could be seen as blessings. It was a line of thought that Frater Solanus had need of soon after his arrival in Milwaukee.

As he entered the training in formal theology in the fall, the academic weaknesses of Frater Solanus were revealed rather quickly. He found philosophy extremely difficult. He wasn't failing, but the downward slide of his grades seemed to predict a trend.

It's likely that these struggles had the same origins as those he'd already experienced. His textbooks were written in Latin, and class discussions were now conducted exclusively in German. Discussing complex theological realities in a language still quite clumsy to his Irish tongue may have been the root of his classroom difficulties.

The director of the Capuchin seminary in Milwaukee was an imposing man. Fr. Anthony Rottensteiner's new class of clerics had already heard a great deal about him through the Capuchin grapevine. He was very demanding, they had heard. By all reports, however, Fr. Anthony would also give struggling but sincere students every benefit of the doubt.

He was, as Frater Solanus and his classmates found, a block of a man with a large wiry gray beard. In the classroom, he was thorough but would sometimes phrase questions so that the answers would be relatively easy to see and deliver. His students discovered that this master scholar was, more often than not, trying to see beyond academic accomplishments into their spirits. For some time, Fr. Anthony had been observing young Casey rather intently. The qualities of Casey as a religious and as a man impressed Fr. Anthony, even if the fellow's scholarly talents didn't.

Anthony himself was an extraordinary scholar in his homeland. When he had asked to join the Capuchins in 1867, the order saw it as an answer from heaven. Someone with Rottensteiner's academic brilliance was needed to oversee the education of seminarians. Fr. Rottensteiner himself had a longing for mission work. But his real mission eventually became guiding young Capuchins to ordination at St. Francis Seminary in Milwaukee. Fr. Rottensteiner was willing to shepherd Frater Solanus through the intricacies of theology discussed in German. Yet, Casey's difficulties could not be overlooked. The impressions the Capuchin superiors had received from the seminary officials at Milwaukee's diocesan seminary seemed to be more and more on their minds.

As always, the spiritual qualities of Frater Solanus were obvious to all. His personality and disposition also seemed to assure that he would blend well in community life. Nonetheless, the academic problems were a mighty stumbling block. A man's personal holiness and gifts could not outweigh academic shortcomings when the priesthood was involved. In addition to ministering, a priest was responsible for interpreting profound and vital theological truths for others. There was very little margin of error in ordaining a man to such a role.

In the autumn of 1899, a year into Solanus Casey's major seminary study, the Capuchin authorities prepared to take a long, hard look at the future of the young man from Superior, Wisconsin.

During the first three semesters of major seminary classes, Frater Solanus stood fifth in a class of six. Behind him, and standing much lower academically, was Frater Damasus Wickland. Ranked fourth, just ahead of Frater Solanus, was another Irishman, Frater John O'Donovan. But unlike Solanus, John knew and spoke German fluently. In the school year of 1899-1900, the men in this class took dogma, moral theology, canon law, Scripture, and liturgy. With the eventual addition of Church history, these courses represented the seminarians' studies until the end of four years of seminary training.

The seminary grading system was a simple breakdown into four levels of academic performance: "1" was a "Good or Very Good" grade, "2" was "Average," "3" was "Passing," and "4" was "Failing." Though Frater Solanus managed to get through each semester with at least a "Passing" (or "3") average, he seemed to be hanging on to that by a shoestring.

While the Capuchin students were doing battle with books inside Milwaukee's St. Francis Seminary, the world outside was welcoming the twentieth century. Britain's Empire under Queen Victoria stretched across the world into five continents. Pope Leo XIII was on the Chair of Peter in Rome and was recognized as one of the most intellectual pontiffs of recent history.

The Capuchin students heard fragments of global and national news, but only such bits and pieces as their superiors passed along. Theirs was a closed world designed to focus attention on a rather narrow field — ordination and spiritual growth. Mail to and from the students was permitted, but, in general, visitors were not. (Frater Solanus had been the beneficiary of one exception to the rule regarding visitors when, not long after his arrival, his brother John and John's new bride, Nell O'Brien Casey, stopped to see him.) Instances of recreation were also rare. But despite this intense concentration, Frater Solanus's academic situation continued to be precarious.

To make their dilemma absolutely clear to him, his superiors and faculty asked him to consider and sign another "attestation," or statement, concerning his eventual ordination. The statement, although written in German, was undoubtedly very well understood this time by Frater Solanus. He read it and signed it on July 5, 1901.

The statement read:

I, Fr. Solanus Casey, having entered the Order with a pure intention and of my own free choice, wish to remain in the Order, and I therefore humbly ask for admission to solemn profession. However, since I do not know whether as a result of my meager talents and defective studies, I am fit to assume the many-sided duties and serious responsibilities of the priesthood, I hereby declare (1) that I do not want to become a priest if my legitimate superiors consider me unqualified; (2) that I still wish to be able to receive one or other of the orders, but will be satisfied if they exclude me entirely from the higher orders. I have offered myself to God without reservation; for that reason I leave it without anxiety to the superiors to decide about me as they may judge best before God.

Solanus thereby once more signed his name to a statement that put his life's hope into someone else's hands.

Just what did this do to a man who had witnessed his parents' yearning to see one of their sons ordained? What did it do to him after he'd obeyed what he saw as God's direction and entered a German order against his own inclinations? How did he feel after he'd entered seminary training late, being humble enough to attend classes with much younger boys, only to find that ordination still might be denied him? At this point, Frater Solanus was already entering his thirties. Since his twenty-first year, he had been struggling to become a priest.

In the journal that he kept for personal reflection, the theme of penance surfaced often in notations for these days. Though his grades edged up, he couldn't see evidence of that incremental improvement making his ordination any more certain.

Fr. Anthony Rottensteiner, director of the seminary, seemed to witness the struggles of young Casey with sympathy. One day, he listened as other seminary teachers discussed ordaining the seminarians to the subdiaconate. Apparently, some of them objected to moving Frater Solanus further along this road toward the priesthood.

But Fr. Anthony disagreed. It was true that Casey's academic troubles were worrisome, he said. But there was something else that this quiet, slender Irishman had. "We shall ordain Frater Solanus," Fr. Anthony predicted, "and, as a priest he will be to the people something like the Curé of Ars." Frater Solanus himself had no such confidence about his eventual ordination.

Living in such anxiety, medical authorities now understand, takes its toll physically as well as emotionally. Sometime during his last years of studies, Solanus began to develop eye trouble. With many hours spent in reading, at least some of it in insufficient light, it should not have been too surprising. His eyes began to really ache. Distressed already by living in a kind of limbo about his future, he became very intimidated by this new difficulty.

Emotionally, he may have felt panicky. His chances for ordination were already jeopardized by his lackluster performance in the classroom. Would there be any chance at all if his superiors thought that he might have serious eye trouble later on? No doubt Solanus did not wish to publicly admit all the trouble his eyes were giving him, but his journal notes for this period betray his fear. The pain of this eyestrain didn't just scare him; he was humbled (and irked!) by the fact that a physical problem like this could so claim the attention of a man supposedly trying to abandon himself to God! That realization bothered him, and the problem began to swirl around in his head.

After a while, however, Frater Solanus decided that he should change his attitude about his ailing eyes. It was apparently a true inspiration. He began to look at his problems in a more positive way, trying to thank the Lord for the blessings he had already received. This new approach was rewarded. "Thanksgiving for same, June 12," he wrote in his journal on that date in 1902. On the following day, he was able to pen, "Consolation on 13th, 1902." Several weeks later, he received minor orders.

Changing his heart, opening himself to let go of some of the worry, and placing his full trust in God were rewarded. Beneath the notes in his journal, a phrase began to appear more and more often: *Deo Gratias* — "Thanks be to God." It was becoming second nature for Frater Solanus to thank God for whatever life was to give to him.

Fr. Anthony may have had a gift when it came to predictions. In February 1903, the seventy-two-year-old seminary director fell ill. He had loved his work with seminarians in the classroom and had once said that if he could not teach, he would die. Five days after he had taught his last class, he died. Feeling a tremendous sense of loss, his seminarians struggled ahead without him.

Four months after the death of Fr. Anthony, Solanus was touched by another death. Opening a letter from home, he read that his first love, Rebecca Tobin, had died at thirty-three. Thinking of the death of the woman he nearly married made him wonder about the mysterious designs heaven creates. In his journal, Solanus wrote simply: "Today, for the first time in seven years, I heard about Rebecca. R.I.P. O queer world and uncertain." To the left of this note about Rebecca, he penned in "*Deo Gratias.*" It was certainly not thanks for the death of a girl he'd loved. Frater Solanus was beginning to understand something very fundamental about God.

Through trials, illnesses, and even losses such as the deaths of Fr. Anthony and of his sweetheart from the past, Solanus could begin to see God's love and goodness. It took a special sort of spiritual vision to see love in life's tragedies and disappointments — but this seminarian, despite trouble with his eyes, was developing the knack for it.

In February, 1904, the Capuchin superiors began to look again at Solanus's grades. It would be the last assessment of his academic standing. In the first semester of his last year of seminary work, his grades in dogma, moral theology, and canon law had improved. He had a passing grade in each of the three. However, although he was not the only student with problems in Scripture and liturgy, the problems were serious. The three students at the bottom of the class were not even given grades in these subjects for this semester.

Anxiety over his ordination was hanging like a heavy gray cloud once again over his head. Solanus wrote to his oldest sister Ellen that although he would "probably be ordained a deacon and priest before August," he still had misgivings that it wouldn't happen. He also told her that he hoped the Holy Spirit would guide his superiors in their decision in all this. But the uncertainty must have been torturous. Instead of his name on this letter, he simply wrote the word "Resignation," with a little cross behind it. When the time came for a decision about the three men lowest in class standing, only a few months remained until the scheduled ordination in July. It was prayerfully determined that all six men in the class were to be ordained to the priesthood. Fr. Anthony's prophecy was already partially correct. Solanus was to be ordained.

Possibly because of his fluid familiarity of German, the superiors decided that Frater John O'Donovan, the fourth in the class, would be ordained with full faculties. His academic average was higher than that of the other two, though not by any great margin, leading some Capuchins to believe later that faculties had initially been withheld from John also, but that he had argued his case successfully to be granted them. He could, after all, certainly hear confessions of German-speaking peoples, who predominated in the areas that the Capuchins served.

Fraters Damasus Wickland and Solanus Casey, on the other hand, were to be ordained as *sacerdotus simplex* — that is, "simplex priests" (or "Mass priests," as they were sometimes called). They were truly and fully priests but could not exercise the faculties of hearing confessions or preaching homilies for congregations. Such a decision was surely as painful for Capuchin superiors as it was to the two men. Nor was it a decision made quickly or casually. To have relatively young, healthy men ordained who could never really make a full pastoral contribution in a parish was a hardship and a loss to the Capuchin community.

Did Damasus and Solanus ever discuss their feelings about the decision with each other or with John O'Donovan? How did the Caseys — Solanus's parents, brothers, and sisters — see this limitation on his priestly role? Such feelings are not recorded, but the loss was surely felt by everyone.

But, at least for one day, those concerns were probably forgotten.

July 24, 1904, was the day that Solanus and his classmates had prayed for. In the vestibule of St. Francis Church in Milwaukee, not far from the classrooms where they had struggled, stood six bearded young men — Fraters Damasus Wickland,

John O'Donovan, Fabian Fetha, Pius Stutzer, Maurus Ascherl, and Solanus Casey. They were about to be ordained by Archbishop Sebastian Messmer, the new bishop of Milwaukee.

"Fr. Solanus" fairly glowed with happiness that day. At thirty-three, he had finally reached a goal set a dozen years earlier. He was a twenty-one-year-old streetcar motorman in Superior, Wisconsin, when the Lord had put him on a new track and moved him in a new direction. If Solanus did not think about this vocation in terms of that sort of metaphor, it would have been surprising.

Exactly one week later, the brand-new "Father" Solanus was again in the vestibule of a familar church. This time, the church was St. Joseph's at Appleton, Wisconsin. A Capuchin regulation required a newly ordained priest to say his "First Mass" in the Capuchin-staffed church closest to his home. Though he was 200 miles from the Caseys still living at Superior, Fr. Solanus joyfully spotted many members of his clan. Among his brothers, Jim, Maurice, and Edward were there. Of course, his parents were there, too. Solanus had not seen his mother, Ellen Casey, in eight years — not since the day he'd left in a blinding snowstorm to take the night train to Detroit to join the order. She may well have seen something different in the face of her now-bearded son, whose hair was already starting to thin on top. Surely, there were signs of a new strength, a new depth of spirit in him.

Though he was not aware of it at the time, Solanus later learned that his father wept for joy through most of his namesake's first Mass. To think that one of his sons was now a priest. The reality was overwhelming for the sixty-four-year-old head of the family!

Maurice, at thirty-six, served at his younger brother's Mass. By then, Maurice was working for the Railroad Mail Service in Chicago and had come up to Appleton for the occasion. Later, in a private moment, Maurice drew his brother away from the crowd of proud family members and friends. Solanus wrote to his oldest brother, James, of the conversation years later:

> Maurice ... brought a tear to my own eye that day when the two of us were strolling in the Monastery garden.... "By George, Barney, I think I'll have to try it over again. I'm getting tired of this blamed rail-roading!"

Though Solanus may have been amused at the light-hearted way that Maurice confessed his plans to study again for the priesthood, he knew that his brother was serious about it. But Solanus himself had only a little time to encourage Maurice and be with his family. Within a day or two, he was to start out for Yonkers, New York. The first "Obedience" received by Fr. Solanus Casey didn't say very much — just that he was to be at Sacred Heart Parish in Yonkers by August 4, 1904.

CHAPTER FIVE

A Priest and Porter
(1904–1918)

On the first few days of August 1904, a newly ordained Fr. Solanus Casey was on a train bound for the East Coast, en route to Yonkers, a suburb of New York City. He'd had little time to linger and relax in Wisconsin after his ordination and first Mass — he had to head east immediately — but the journey itself might have been some small vacation for the thirty-three-year-old Fr. Casey. As a former streetcar motorman, he was at home with the back-and-forth jostling, the train's full-throttle rhythm.

The black-bearded Capuchin likely had his face to the window most of the way. He had never been east of Detroit. The state of Ohio, the Allegheny Mountains of Pennsylvania, the states of New Jersey and New York, were all new to him. As the train rolled away mile after mile of his native Midwest, Solanus admired the farmers' fields. It was the same good ground his parents may have crossed in their journey west, almost forty years earlier. Now, their son was headed to New York City, a city reputed to be the second largest in the world. Only London, with more than four million people, outranked New York City in size.

It was not outranked in hustle and bustle, however. Turn-of-the-century New York was a vigorous city. New immigrants from Italy, Greece, and Eastern Europe now challenged the dominance of the Irish, Germans, and Scandinavians. With them came new ghettos, new foods, new ways. It was also a time of the Wall Street speculators and of opulence and conspicuous consumption for those lucky enough to inherit the fortunes of the previous generation's so-called "robber barons." It was the decade of the infamous sweatshops, too, culminating in the terrible Triangle Shirtwaist Factory fire of 1911 that claimed 146 lives.

If the young Capuchin's eyes grew wide at the fertile stretch of Pennsylvania valleys, the city of New York must have seemed a miracle of twentieth-century life! New York at the turn of the century was the showcase of American progress and political clout. For decades, Tammany Hall, a Democratic political organization, had heavily influenced New York politics. There was even a New Yorker, Theodore Roosevelt, in the White House.

Fr. Solanus could not take his eyes off the elevated trains in the city. With the elevated and surface trains, this city carried more paying passengers during a year's time than all the steam railroads of North and South America together. Solanus may have also noticed that the automobiles he saw were moving, stopping, and starting in a rather precise manner. Four years before, in the first year of the new century, New York had instituted its first traffic regulations, in spite of the outcry from "freedom-loving" New Yorkers.

He couldn't see what was happening in the "bowels of the earth"— that New Yorkers were going mad over the newest form of traveling: the subway. Beginning at City Hall Station, to Grand Central, across Times Square, to the end of the line at 145th Street, it was a great way to spend a day — for only a nickel!

New York was also boasting of its remarkable new "skyscrapers." A building called the "Flatiron Building" had been completed three years before, in 1901, in this city.

Making his way past these "big city" wonders, Fr. Solanus headed toward Sacred Heart Friary in Yonkers. Founded thirteen years before, the gray granite monastery stood on a hilltop overlooking the Hudson River. Solanus was happy to discover that his own sparsely furnished room had a good view of the river. The scene reminded him, he wrote later, of the rolling Mississippi and his early childhood near Prescott.

Solanus was barely settled when he was summoned by the monastery's superior, seventy-three-year-old Fr. Bonaventure Frey. Fr. Bonaventure was fully aware of the unusual circumstances that Solanus presented to him. Bonaventure was the co-founder of the Capuchin order in America and had established Sacred Heart Friary and Parish.

In 1856, Fr. Bonaventure had come with Fr. Francis Haas from Switzerland with almost no money between them. But their struggle to establish monasteries, to found an American province, had been successful. By 1883, the year St. Bonaventure Monastery was begun in Detroit, seven monasteries, most with parishes, had been founded in Wisconsin and New York. As Fr. Bonaventure contemplated the fine Irish features of Solanus Casey, he may have been thinking of his own life. Appearing before him now was a man, still quite young, whose apparent potential as an active Capuchin would be severely limited. Though he could and would perform baptisms and officiate at weddings, Solanus Casey could not really be assigned to Sacred Heart Parish. He lacked the faculties of preaching doctrinal sermons and of hearing confessions. With great kindness, Fr. Bonaventure finally told the newcomer that his assigned duties would be acting as sacristan and supervising altar boys in the parish. Traditionally, such roles were not given to ordained priests but to the Capuchin brothers.

Perhaps not until this day and hour did Solanus realize what his limited faculties would mean. In seminary days, he had dreamed of becoming a missionary, but with limitations on him, he could never be given a missionary assignment, even though he had studied philosophy, canon law, dogma, Scripture, liturgy, and moral theology for ten years. With no bitterness and no brooding that anyone could note, he graciously embraced his "assignments."

The Capuchins of Sacred Heart Parish pose with some of the students in Yonkers, New York. This photo, taken about 1912, shows Fr. Solanus in the middle of the back row.

But very quickly, the friars noted, Fr. Solanus Casey familiarized himself with the church and learned the locations and proper care of Sacred Heart's altar linens, priestly vestments, Mass articles, altar breads and wine, candlesticks, and flower vases. And he began to meet with the lively lineup of elementary schoolboys to serve Masses at Sacred Heart Church, which occupied the first floor of one wing of the friary.

Edward, one of the Casey brothers, wrote to Solanus when he heard the details of his older brother's first assignment. Always something of a poet, Edward put into verse his respect for Barney's humble acceptance of his tasks. He wrote a short poem called "The Brother Sacristan." In the poem, a "modest figure kneels to pay the voiceless homage of his heart" and then "silently from place to place he steals / the worship of his fingers to impart."

Solanus treasured the poem. But he also treasured the chance to be in such close proximity with the Blessed Sacrament. He was very precise and devout in this role; a remarkable spirituality had taken root in him, and here — working near the altar — it continued.

From another brother, Maurice, Solanus soon learned that the words about studying for the priesthood had not been carelessly spoken. Though almost thirty-eight, Maurice had located a seminary in Kitchener, Ontario; he planned to try the seminary work and then join a religious order — perhaps the Capuchins — later. Solanus was delighted, especially since he knew that his brother Edward was also planning to become a priest. Three Casey priests! Solanus knew his father would be in his glory!

Sacred Heart's young acolytes, on the other hand, often made him wonder how his father had managed with so many boys. Solanus had the responsibility of drilling the altar boys to memorize the Latin responses at Mass. He also had to see that they showed up for Mass on time and piously performed their duties at the altar.

To get to know them and to win their trust, Solanus would often organize field trips for his gang of Mass servers. Ice cream sodas always capped the trips, but visits to a church along the way were invariably included to "set a good example." Slender but wiry, Fr. Solanus also impressed the boys when they played baseball together. Sometimes he would bat fly balls for them or hit them grounders to see if they were any good as shortstops. When he played in a game, he was always the catcher, refusing to wear the catcher's mask, and played in his habit. He played the game with gusto. The boys loved him for his wild courage as well as for his kind concern for them.

But despite their affection for him, Sacred Heart's altar boys groaned when they found themselves scheduled to serve Mass for Fr. Solanus. Slow with the Mass prayers and still cautious with his Latin, Fr. Solanus took more time with his Mass than any of the other priests, and those Masses seemed to take forever.

In 1906, a change took place at Sacred Heart that affected the assignments of Fr. Solanus. Fr. Bonaventure decided to retire. He was over seventy-five and, apparently, growing deaf and blind. After long years in service to the Capuchin order and in dedication to the Church, he wished to simply live and work at the parish as any other priest. The responsibilities of pastor and superior of the house then went to Fr. Aloysius Blonigen, who added to the mission of Fr. Solanus Casey. From that point, Fr. Solanus was to take on the added task of being the friary porter.

In general, monastery porters were religious brothers. Theirs was the daily "glory" of answering the doorbell, running for far-flung friars when visitors arrived, and handing on messages, packages, and occasional complaints. A porter might meet dozens of people each week. For the thirty-five-year-old Fr. Solanus Casey, the additional assignment was to have unforeseen blessings.

Sacred Heart Parish soon began to know "Fr. Solanus" in a new way. There were a half-dozen ethnic groups in the parish who spoke little or no English. But the porter's kind blue eyes and smile translated into every language. They saw him sweeping the sidewalks in front of the monastery and feeding the hungry who stopped there. And he was invariably on the scene at Sacred Heart's traditional Labor Day picnic. It was easy to see that he loved the fun, the beer, the talk, and hot dogs with onions. He was an easy man to approach, and yet the priestly status of this very approachable priest didn't make any sense to many of Sacred Heart's people. They couldn't understand why he did the jobs usually done by religious brothers, when he was a priest. After visitors had confided in Solanus and had benefited from his easy counsel and prayers, they often asked him to hear their confessions.

"I can't do that," Fr. Solanus would respond softly. Instead, with little or no explanation, he would advise them to seek the sacrament from one of the other priests. Few if any of the folks in contact with the monastery would have heard of the term "simplex priest." A priest was a priest and did the things priests always do, they presumed.

With the exception of occasional *ferverinos* — inspirational talks — Fr. Solanus, who seemed to be a deeply spiritual man, was not to be seen preaching at the pulpit. And he was never to be found hearing confessions at the church. No one outside of the monastery had any idea why. Finally, some of the parishioners came to an interesting conclusion.

"Fr. Solanus loves God so much that he cannot hear confessions," they began to say. "He might not be able to take it if he discovered how many people are hurting God!"

If the predictable patterns of priestly ministry were more limited for Solanus Casey, however, other means of serving — extraordinary means — were not. Acting as porter, he opened the door, so to speak, to something very unexpected, something very good. "Favors" and "blessings" — that is what the youngish simplex priest called these events.

As early as 1901, even before ordination, Solanus had begun to record the circumstances of answered prayers. In part, this practice was mandated. Seminarians were expected to keep a spiritual journal.

Years later, after he was assigned to Sacred Heart, one of the notations Solanus made in this journal had to do with "altar boy trouble." In the long run, being distressed by sloppy service from boys may seem foolish. But for Solanus, it was not foolish. Seeing to it that the boys served well on the altar was a good share of his priestly assignment.

Fr. Casey had decided years before that he was not going to do any part of his given jobs with less than one-hundred-percent devotion. A notebook notation finally recorded an answer to his prayer for better servers who would behave. Following a novena to the Immaculate Conception, concluded on December 8, her feast, Fr. Solanus wrote, "Good boys asked to be servers!"

A minor miracle? A small, but happy, coincidence? Solanus simply labeled all such occurrences and much more dramatic ones as "blessings." They all had one and the same name and came from one and the same source. That was the understanding with which he increasingly lived and worked.

A photo taken during this era shows Solanus posing with his charges in front of Sacred Heart. Twenty-six serious-looking boys, immaculately attired in surplices and cassocks, stand at attention with their director Fr. Solanus and with Fr. Anscar, the superior.

As the Sacred Heart porter, Solanus had begun to meet more and more people. There were Germans, Irish, and Italians. Many of the Italians were newly immigrated and needed an understanding friend, though Solanus would send for an interpreter in order to "understand" them. When they called for him or referred to him, Fr. Solanus Casey was "the Holy Priest." When visitors talked with him, they apparently found

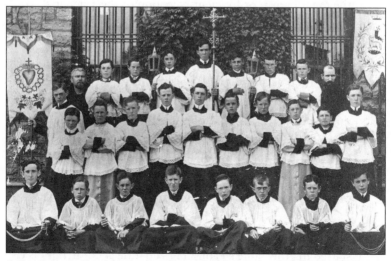

Father Solanus (far right, back row) poses with the altar boys he shepherded at Sacred Heart Parish in Yonkers, around 1912.

nothing really remarkable in what he said. In fact, he was invariably low-key. Solanus would welcome them, and then invite them to be seated with him in one of the small parlors. Mostly, he simply listened. Then he would close his eyes or look off into space as if to see into the issue more deeply. Only after the contemplation and quiet discernment would the bright blue eyes focus once again on the troubled individual seated in front of him.

The counsel that so many found comforting was inevitably very simple. He would ask them a few questions, pray with them, and finally suggest that they thank God for blessings already received and those they would receive in the future. Also, Solanus would often suggest that his visitors show some sign of gratitude for the Lord's goodness.

He would ask for more frequent use of the sacraments, especially penance and the Eucharist, quoting Pope St. Pius X, the great patron of frequent reception of the Eucharist. And, sometimes, he would ask if those seeking prayers would like to support the Capuchins' Seraphic Mass Association.

The "SMA," as the Capuchins dubbed it, was established about 1900 as a result of a Swiss woman's inspiration. Desiring to help the Capuchins, she suggested that the association might solicit donations for their foreign missions with the promise of remembrance through prayers and Masses. The Capuchins in the United States therefore promoted the SMA at each friary. In general, however, there was little aggressive promotion and, as a result, only minimal donations.

But after Fr. Solanus began to answer the doors at Sacred Heart in 1906, SMA donations coming in from Yonkers started to grow quite steadily. He said little about it, but his visitors gradually talked. They talked and talked about their prayers, the SMA commitment, and the fact that their prayers were being answered! In fact, prayers began to be answered at a rate that gained attention. Solanus had more and more requests to visit the sick down in the valleys.

Years later, a Sister of St. Agnes, Sister Agrippina (Carmella) Petrosino related that, as a young girl, she acted as translator for Solanus. She lived in the Italian neighborhood within the parish. On one occasion, Carmella's mother sent her to get Fr. Solanus for a woman who'd become ill soon after delivering a child.

"As soon as Father came in, he asked for holy water," Sister Agrippina remembered. "But they had no holy water. Fr. Solanus said, 'Oh, poor, poor, poor.' I ran over to our house and got some. When I came back, he prayed over her, blessed her and from then on the woman got over her infection and lived a long time afterwards."

On another day, an Italian woman who knew Mrs. Petrosino asked her to have her little girl bring Fr. Solanus. The woman had suffered from severe headaches for years. When he arrived, the woman asked him to simply place his hand on her head. He did that as he recited some prayers from a prayerbook. The woman apparently got better, Sister Aggripina theorized, because she never again sought help from Solanus.

While walking along with his young Italian translator some time later, Fr. Solanus asked the girl what she hoped to be when she grew up.

"I'd like to be a Sister of St. Agnes," she told him.

"You will be," Fr. Solanus assured her with a smile.

Even those already serving as Sisters of St. Agnes paid attention to the remarks Fr. Solanus made about the future. The nuns told one another, "If, in June, when you go back to the Motherhouse in Wisconsin, Fr. Solanus says, 'See you in September,' you will be coming back; if he just says 'Goodbye,' you will be transferred."

Fr. Casey, his fellow friars noted, seemed to grow more assured about many things. The thing he seemed most confident about was the unending and boundless love of God. When Solanus did have the chance to give small *ferverinos*, it was usually for the groups he helped to direct at Sacred Heart.

Before addressing groups, he prepared diligently. He always loved to write, and he was a very effective writer. English and composition had been his best subjects during school days. Pages of notes and jotted scraps of ideas would fill notebook pages before he finally wrote his talks. When the little homily was done, the message typically touched on God's love for his children. It was the first fundamental in the spiritual consciousness of Solanus. Learning to accept that love and respond to it, in his eyes, constituted the challenge of Christian life. His messages to groups or individuals seen in counseling were seldom more complicated than that.

In 1910, Solanus had the chance to repeat some of those themes for a special friend. Paul Francis Wattson, an Anglican, had founded an Anglican community of friars based on the Franciscan rule at Garrison, New York, about twenty-five miles north of Yonkers. Solanus met him and encouraged him. Finally, Wattson converted to Catholicism and studied for the priesthood, and his religious community, the Friars of the Atonement, followed his path. Paul Wattson was so impressed with Solanus that he chose him to preach the homily at his first Mass on July 3, 1910.

Toward the end of the year, Fr. Solanus made note of his fortieth birthday with a reference in his journal.

November 25th '10, (40 Anniversary)
Birth Day Present and surprise after
long drought a gentle though copious Rain
& after, beautiful Thanksgiving-Day, *Deo Gratias*.

There was no other recognition of it, with the possible exception of greetings from the family, for a couple of reasons. First, instead of birthdays, the friar's name day — the feast of the saint whose name the friar had received at investiture — was celebrated. Second, due to a clerical error made when he entered fourteen years earlier, Fr. Solanus's birthday was thought to be October 25 rather than November 25.

In June 1911, Fr. Solanus traveled to another ordination, that of his brother Maurice, in St. Paul, Minnesota. He could remember seeing Maurice leave home to go to the seminary the first time in 1883. He was thirteen, Maurice sixteen. Solanus rejoiced that his brother's dream was now finally fulfilled in the Lord. At ordination, Maurice was forty-three years old.

Two years later, in the fall of 1913, Ellen and Bernard Casey Sr. marked their golden wedding anniversary. Their ten sons and four daughters decided to gather together to celebrate the joy and fruitfulness of their parents. But the gathering had to take place in Washington State. In the early years of the century, six of the Casey boys had moved west, as had Ellen, the oldest child, and her husband. With so many of their children in the Seattle area, the parents soon followed.

So Solanus went to talk with the superior of Sacred Heart and asked permission to travel across the country. This was no small request: travel from New York to Seattle covered 3,025 miles. With a week-long celebration set aside for the October 6 anniversary, and another week needed for the journey back, he would have to be gone for the better part of a month. But he had also been faithfully serving at Sacred Heart for nine years, and permission was quickly given. Some other friars would answer the door, shepherd the altar boys, lay out the altar linens each day, and meet with the groups Solanus served as chaplain.

And so, on an autumn day in 1913, Fr. Solanus hiked his street-length cassock up a bit and stepped up into a passenger train. The black-bearded, brown-robed Capuchin drew plenty of curious glances as he made his way down the aisles. He smiled to the right and left and greeted a few folk. Having little luggage, he settled into a seat quickly to begin the longest sightseeing trip of his forty-two years.

The cross-country journey was exciting for a man who'd never traveled much west of the Mississippi River. Across the Plains states, through the Rockies, up through the northwest to Seattle, Solanus thoroughly enjoyed the scenery as well as

Bernard and Ellen Casey are shown surrounded by their family at the couple's golden wedding anniversary celebration, October 6, 1913, in Seattle.

the people he met and spoke with along the way. But he looked forward most of all to spending time with his family, especially his parents, whom he hadn't seen in years.

Since his move to New York, he'd also had little time to talk to his two ordained brothers. Edward, younger than Solanus by nine years, was ordained at age thirty-two — in 1912, the year after Maurice became a priest. All three brothers would have a role in the Mass that marked their parents' anniversary; Fr. Solanus was to give the homily.

In Seattle, surrounded by their children and grandchildren (thirty-four in all), Bernard Sr. and Ellen rejoiced in the blessings their fifty years together had brought. This was a theme that their son, Fr. Solanus, was to use as well. In the anniversary homily, he

This photo, taken in 1913 in Seattle, shows the three Casey brothers who became priests. From left, Fr. Maurice (ordained in 1911), Fr. Edward (ordained in 1912), and Fr. Solanus (ordained in 1904).

spoke to all about the gratitude that should be given to God for past blessings to his mother and father. Weaving the joys and challenges of his parents' lives on their Wisconsin homestead through his remarks, he pointed out that it was also good and just to thank God at any given moment for blessings to be given in the future. Fr. Solanus made it clear to the family that even hurts and illnesses were, therefore, properly viewed as blessings. Through the burdens of life, as he had learned in his simplex priesthood, God works His will.

His message apparently touched his parents and his brothers and sisters deeply. They spoke of it at length, and there were some tears. They saw in this son and brother a deeper and deeper faith, a spiritual gift that had grown in the years during which he'd been so far away from them all.

If the joy of the reunion week was great, however, the pain of separation also loomed large. The Caseys realized that no other occasion could gather them all together again. They took time to talk, to play, to eat, to reminisce. Then, when the festivities were over, Solanus boarded a train once again and headed east, back to New York, where he had another important commitment to Sacred Heart Parish.

Previously, the members of Sacred Heart had met and attended Mass in one of the first-floor wings of the friary. Now, in 1913, the parish was dedicating its church. Solanus knew he should be back to see the new structure dedicated, and he wanted to be sure he was with his parish for the event.

With tight travel scheduling, however, he was in great danger of missing the dedication ceremonies. But somehow, Fr. Solanus knew that he was meant to celebrate the parish event, just as he had been able to celebrate his family's reunion.

On the way home, he wanted to offer Mass at a parish church in St. Paul, Minnesota. But as the train pulled into the city, the conductor shook his head at the slender priest's inquiry and told him that the only train headed for Chicago would be leaving within thirty minutes. He would have to stay in the station if he expected to be on it.

Solanus needed to be on that Chicago train if he was to be home in Yonkers on time — at least in theory. But he also knew in his heart that he should say Mass on this fall Friday morning.

So, leaving a puzzled conductor behind him and grabbing his skimpy suitcase, he left the train and walked off in a light rain to St. Mary's Church. There, he offered his Mass with the same conscientious care and attention that he always took.

Sure enough, when he arrived back at the train station, Fr. Solanus found that his Chicago-bound train was only then chugging into the depot. It had been delayed.

In Detroit, he repeated the "risk" to say Mass at St. Bonaventure's, where he had entered the Capuchin novitiate . . . with the same happy result.

To the great joy of the parishioners, Fr. Solanus arrived at Sacred Heart in time to see the celebration through. The Italians, Irish, and Germans who made up the people of Sacred Heart Parish knew that their celebration would have been incomplete without him; the "Holy Priest" was clearly a gift to the community, and his presence made this family gathering a full one.

In 1914, Fr. Solanus had already completed ten years of service to Sacred Heart in Yonkers. In that decade, his gifts for relating to the troubled and the sick had begun to emerge, all beginning with his ministry of answering the door and greeting visitors. But as the years passed, he seemed to hear a call to move out of the friary and knock on doors himself.

Offering friendship and prayers for those bedridden or in pain, Fr. Solanus began a habit of calling on parishioners, carrying holy water and a crucifix with him. He made special efforts to reach out to those of other faiths, especially Jews and Protestants. It was an unusual gesture for the day, but Solanus had carefully observed this ecumenical effort in Fr. Stephen Eckert in 1904, the year the two had lived together at Sacred Heart.

In 1914, the world at large was on the edge of World War
I. In late June, the archduke of Austria, Francis Ferdinand, and
his wife, Sophie, were assassinated. Declarations of war followed within weeks from Germany, Austria, Russia, France,
Britain, and Italy. In the Vatican, Pius X spent his summer —
and his spirit — trying to reestablish peace. His efforts failed,
and the seventy-nine-year-old pontiff died on August 20. Soon
after, Pope Benedict XV came to the Chair of St. Peter.

In New York, the military stretched a steel net across the
narrows of New York Harbor to prevent German subs from
entering. Unfortunately, the city's German-Americans also suffered from anti-German sentiment.

As radio and telegraph began to speed the news of world
events, war talk spilled over into Yonkers, into Sacred Heart
Parish. Adding to the mix of immigrants from Germany and
Italy, Irish immigrants often had strong feelings about the con-
flicts as well, because of a widespread hostility toward Britain.
And so, new needs for healing and reconciliation continued to
draw Fr. Solanus.

The pain being felt in Europe was compounded for the
Caseys by the news that the head of the clan was ill. Bernard
James Casey died at seventy-five years of age in 1915, in Seattle, after a lengthy and painful illness. He had died, Fr. Solanus
was later told, saying a prayer to Our Lady of Sorrows. For
Solanus, there wasn't time to go across the country to attend
the funeral. He prayed for his father — and his mother — at
Sacred Heart, then sat down and wrote letters of consolation
to his mother.

Many letters postmarked from Yonkers also went to Maurice — or Fr. Maurice Joachim, as he was now called — during this time. Soon after ordination in 1911, he was assigned

as pastor for a massive mission territory in Montana. His mission, under the jurisdiction of the diocese of St. Paul, included eleven tiny parishes. One hundred miles separated the parishes at the extremities of his mission area. In between and surrounding them was breathtakingly beautiful scenery, though it seemed to matter very little to Fr. Maurice Joachim.

His brother, Solanus knew well, was not happy in his ministry. Edward had written to tell him about it. Longing for the companionship and the bustle of the city, their older brother grew more and more morose. Solanus tried to share his vision of finding joy wherever God placed him, but Fr. "Maurice J." continued to suffer from despondency.

On the third day of January in 1916, Fr. Solanus wrote to his sister, Margaret, that he was still having trouble throwing off a severe chest cold. "I must try and answer your pleasant letter and beautiful boquet [*sic*] received this morning with one from Leo also.... Not that I am exactly sick, but I've had a touch of le grippe these few days with quite a cold in the chest and head. The latter cold seems softer since reading these letters...." The chatty note went on to refer to the view of the Hudson that he had from his room and to his happiness with his vocation and work there in New York, despite his inability to see more of the family. The letter was not mailed until two days later, when Solanus added to it and sent it off, noting that he'd fallen asleep before finishing it and, later, was too busy to get it into the mail.

In the spring of 1918, Ellen Casey developed pneumonia in Seattle. Letters from the "western Caseys" told Fr. Solanus of their mother's failing health. Frs. Maurice Joachim, from Montana, and Edward, from St. Paul, traveled west to see her. For Fr. Solanus, however, the trip was out of the question.

Ellen Murphy Casey could not relinquish her role as mother even during her last days. When Edward walked into her room, she asked him, "Fr. Edward, did you have any supper?" On May 2, she died at the age of seventy-four, surrounded by many of her children, including Frs. Edward and Maurice Joachim.

In June, Solanus made a notation in his notebook about an added responsibility at Sacred Heart Parish.

> June 16, 1918. Today appointed and permitted to be "Director of League" (after trying at least, to direct it for about ten years. *Deo Gratias!*)

It was a privilege to officially direct the Sacred Heart League, according to Fr. Solanus, even though he had already been performing the service for ten years. This "privilege," however, was short-lived.

Several months after his mother's death, Solanus learned that he would be leaving Sacred Heart. A triennial chapter in Detroit had worked out assignments for the entire province. On the day he learned of the change, he was already packing to leave.

His new assignment was to be at the Capuchin parish called Our Lady of Sorrows. Probably the sting of leaving was blunted by his transfer to a parish dedicated to the Mother of God. In his long years at Sacred Heart, his boyhood devotion to the Blessed Mother had simply grown wider and deeper. He said his daily Rosary with great devotion and advised others to do the same.

A book called *The Mystical City of God* by Mary of Agreda, a Spanish mystic, also had a powerful impact on him during his

Sacred Heart years. In the book, the writer described the "life of Mary." Solanus found it a rich source for contemplating Mary's role in salvation.

The work had mixed reviews within the Church. It, in fact, had been condemned ninety years earlier, due to some statements which theologians saw as extreme; Rome questioned (among other things) the author's assertion that anyone who denied its contents committed a sin. In light of statements like that, Pope Clement XIV stopped Mary of Agreda's beatification process in 1771. But, despite criticism of her written work, she was acknowledged as a woman of great holiness.

Fr. Solanus knew of this controversy but was also aware that *The Mystical City of God* was treasured by many churchmen in his own time. He saw the work primarily as a tool of inspiration and devotion, and that was how he recommended it to people who came to him for spiritual counseling.

"I am just about to leave Yonkers for a new field, down in the very heart of the metropolis," he wrote to his sister, Margaret, on July 16. "In a way I almost feel sad to leave the Sacred Heart Monastery and Parish where I've been laboring (if laboring is the right word) for close to fourteen years. Well now, 'Goodbye' for the present from Yonkers. My new address will be 213 Stanton Street, New York City, New York."

Packing his few clothes, several books, a rosary or two, some pens, and his violin, the forty-seven-year-old Fr. Solanus tucked Margaret's letter into his pocket to mail later. Soon, he was investigating the streetcar schedule to make his way south to Manhattan. He said a quick goodbye to Sacred Heart, though few there yet knew that they were losing the Capuchin whom the Italians unabashedly called their "Holy Priest."

CHAPTER SIX

An Outbreak of "Special Favors" (1918–1924)

FR. SOLANUS HAD NO PROBLEM finding his way downtown into Manhattan and over to Our Lady of Sorrows, at Pitt and Stanton Streets. He also knew that he would surely find his way in whatever new ministry his new superior would give to him. Our Lady of Sorrows Parish was well established. It had been founded in 1867, and the Capuchins were at home there. Nonetheless, he probably couldn't also help but think of what he had left behind.

He had been at Sacred Heart for fourteen years. He had moved through his first years of priesthood, through his thirties and into his forties. The tasks and responsibilities had grown throughout his years there. He had made friends in Yonkers, and many people found a friend in him.

On this July day in 1918, Solanus found himself at a new door, and a new beginning, once again. He rang the bell at Our Lady of Sorrows and waited for some brother Capuchin to open it, a task he had done so many times himself at Sacred Heart. But as he waited, he may have wondered what tasks were already being set aside on the other side of the door for a middle-aged simplex priest.

Soon enough, Solanus learned that his days at Our Lady of Sorrows would be less regimented. He was not given the job of porter, but was to act as director for the parish altar boys again. And, he was also given the role of moderating the Young Ladies' Sodality.

As Fr. Casey settled into life in Manhattan in those early autumn weeks, the First World War was drawing to a close. Though American troops had only entered the war in 1917, more than 75,000 U.S. service personnel had been killed. In addition, more than 200,000 had been wounded, were missing, or were prisoners of war. Two million American men had been sent to France, and another two million were in training in the U.S., when the Armistice ending the war was signed on November 11. Peace would return to the world, though Solanus and thousands of other Irish-Americans were concerned about the state of affairs in Ireland.

To Solanus personally, however, came a new opportunity for peace. Without the responsibilities of counseling people, he was left with more time to spend quietly. He chose to study Scripture and read more diligently, spending his time reading or rereading the Fathers of the Church, the lives of the saints, and the writings of the mystics. Books were stacked up in his small room. Notes on what he was reading began to fill up his notebooks. In what could have seemed to be an embarrassing lack of "real responsibility" or "real work," he saw an opportunity to grow spiritually. And this kind of growth took time.

During the months that followed, he would frequently make his way to the monastery chapel to pray in the presence of the Blessed Sacrament. Contemplation had always been a favorite form of prayer for him, but now, because he was reading and studying more about it, he found it even more attractive. He read and reread the works of St. Catherine of Siena, St. Bernard, and others. In addition to the powerful silence and prayer he was reading about, a powerful exchange was apparently continuing and deepening between Fr. Solanus and his God. Until 1921, there were few notations of any kind about him or his ministry at Our Lady of Sorrows, almost as though his presence there was a secret. But in 1921, the monastery journal reported Fr. Solanus's hospitalization after he developed some kind of gangrenous infection which quickly became painful and dangerous. At fifty, he was operated on for the first time in his life.

The emergency surgery took place at St. Francis Hospital on a Sunday morning, after Fr. Solanus endured a night of excruciating pain. When it was over, he wrote about the illness in a letter to his sister, Margaret LeDoux, in California.

"I had been in agony for at least 40 hours though no one seemed to know it," he wrote. "While I tried to thank God for it all, my principal prayer — at least a thousand times repeated — was 'God help us.'" Only as he came out of the anaesthetic and dimly saw that the doctors were completing their work could he again pray, "*Deo Gratias*! Thanks be to God!"

It was a lesson in pain and helplessness that probably could not have been provided to an individual without this sort of personal suffering. As the ordeal concluded and his infection and pain receded, Solanus thanked God again and again — not only because he'd had only a short stay in the hospital, but because he had been able to say Mass every day, even during the most painful hours.

Later in the same year, on October 21, 1921, Fr. Solanus learned that he was being transferred again. This time he was to move to Our Lady, Queen of Angels Parish (sometimes simply called Queen of Angels Parish or Our Lady of the Angels Parish), located in Harlem. This ended his quiet three-year assignment at Our Lady of Sorrows; the monastery log at Sorrows merely noted on October 25 that Fr. Solanus Casey was going to Queen of Angels, while a Fr. Cajetan was coming from Harlem to Our Lady of Sorrows. It was an even exchange of men. As usual, there was no explanation for the change of assignment. Assignments were a matter of obedience, not discussion. On the same day he learned of his transfer, Solanus packed up and headed for 113th Street and Third Avenue in Harlem.

If he expected to continue with the same ministries at his new parish, however, he was soon to discover that changes were planned for him. At Queen of Angels, he was told he was not to act as sacristan, director of altar boys, or chaplain for the Young Ladies' Sodality. Solanus, not quite fifty-one years old, was to have only one assignment there. But this assignment was to be a demanding one.

Though he was given the title of monastery porter to assure his easy and constant contact with people in need of help, his actual task was to spend his time in pastoral work — and also to be the promoter of the Seraphic Mass Association. Obviously, the work that Fr. Solanus did years earlier, at Sacred Heart, had made an impression on the provincial superiors. Perhaps his time at Our Lady of Sorrows was intended to test him — or, perhaps, to provide him with an opportunity to deepen his spiritual roots.

Capuchin superiors knew very well that a man restless for the daily dynamics of meeting and counseling people risked being less well-grounded in spiritual realities. Solanus, on the other hand, had rejoiced in his quiet time, and time for prayer, at Our Lady of Sorrows. There was no chafing under his enforced assignment to "inactivity," to silence. He grew because of it, which was easy to see.

The truth was that the province of St. Joseph had never seen a Capuchin quite like this soft-spoken, Wisconsin-born Casey. His superiors knew that he would have to be guided under the vow of obedience by which he was bound. And yet, it was also clear that great gifts operated through him. Those gifts, they knew, should not be quenched. God seemed to want to work in a special way through this man whom they had ordained with only limited faculties.

So, the new porter settled in to a front office, provided for his use, and began to answer the door at Our Lady of the Angels. People who came to seek his help typically wanted to talk for a while. In a very natural and quite spontaneous way, Solanus began to see and counsel people all day long. No appointments were made. People simply came, lined up inside and outside of the front office, and finally poured out their problems to him. Just as he had at Sacred Heart, he handled those who came to him simply and directly.

On his desk, Fr. Solanus had a book for enrollment in the Seraphic Mass Association (SMA). When he thought it was appropriate, he would ask those seeking answers to receive the sacraments more often, or to seek God more enthusiastically in prayer. In the process, he would also ask if he could enroll them in the SMA. He was an official promoter for the Seraphic Mass Association and he believed in it completely. By asking for participation in the SMA, he was actually trying to draw out some sign of expectant faith.

That seemed to be crucial for him. If the petitioners would agree to commit themselves, he would methodically enroll their names, addresses, and intentions in careful, legible script in the SMA enrollment book. As at Sacred Heart, the book began to fill. The usual charge of fifty cents for annual enrollment was collected unless Solanus could see that he would cause a hardship to ask for it. Through the autumn and winter of 1921 and into the new year, the pattern and the procedures continued more or less unchanged. The people came with troubled marriages, threats of dangerous surgeries, estranged children, dying mothers, unemployment, or alcohol-related problems in this era of Prohibition. There were literally hundreds of concerns to take to heart and to prayer.

Solanus seemed to handle each need, each set of worried eyes, delicately but effectively. He radiated a sense that God cared about all those things. He often laid hands on those sick and prayed for a healing then and there. And his promises of prayer for individual intentions were more than polite words. He began to spend extended time in the chapel after office hours and his Capuchin house commitments were fulfilled.

As the weeks went by, many people would return to the monastery with a certain lift in their step, with a light in their eyes. They waited in line for their turn, interspersed among worried and weary petitioners. They came to tell the slender porter that there had been a healing, a reconciliation, a job placement, a miracle! Prayers were being answered.

Fr. Solanus would listen to the good news. He rejoiced in the joy of prayers being answered. His blue eyes would light up above a smile wreathed in his graying beard. Then, invariably, he would remind his happy visitors that thanks were due only to God, only to the prayers and intercessions of many Capuchin priests who had remembered their intentions in Masses. He would urge a continuing devotion to the sacraments and prayer

— an earnest faith. "And thank God," he reminded everyone, showing happy people to the monastery door.

On January 4, 1922, at a special Mass and celebration, Fr. Solanus celebrated twenty-five years in the Capuchin order. He was very new to this parish, but no one would have thought so. A somewhat playful entry in the monastery's chronicle for the day described the outpouring of affection for Fr. Solanus: "A great multitude of the population of New York" had called to greet him, the logbook noted. A quarter-century earlier, on that day, a restless twenty-six-year-old had finally found a measure of peace when the brown Franciscan habit was slipped over his head — even though in the weeks prior to that day, he had been tempted to leave St. Bonaventure, leave the Capuchins, and leave Detroit!

In the years that followed that long-ago January day in 1897, the first part of his given religious name, "Francis," was almost forgotten. He was known simply as Frater Solanus and later as Fr. Solanus. But the brown hooded habit with the white knotted cord seemed to fit him perfectly right from the start. In it, and in his life as a Capuchin friar, he would become more and more comfortable.

After the twenty-fifth-year celebration, the friars' house at Queen of Angels returned more or less to normal. The lines of people seeking to talk with Fr. Solanus grew still longer. But by now, that seemed to be the normal, predictable result of the doorkeeper's remarkable gifts.

Often, Fr. Solanus could be seen protesting to those whose prayers had been answered. He would insist that such "favors" could be given from God's hands, no matter who had enrolled the petitioner in the SMA. Nonetheless, province directors noted that very few claims for healings or answered prayers seemed to originate from other SMA enrollments in other monasteries.

In September 1922, Fr. Solanus sat down at an old typewriter and labored over a letter unlike any others he'd written during the year. He was outraged at two editorials printed in the *Catholic News* about the Irish-British situation. When it came to this subject of Irish oppression, Fr. Solanus's gentleness and easygoing docility became replaced with fire, as the editors of the *Catholic News* soon discovered. Over this subject and other "social justice" topics, he could become very assertive and impassioned.

In five typed pages, he poured out a tirade against Britain's "Ireland policies":

> If Britain is in favor of the said "Free State" — and she seems to mightily so — then, honest, unselfish lovers of Ireland, and of truth, and of justice, ought to be opposed to it.

He referred to "Britain-broken Treaties" and British hypocrisy and went on to state:

> . . . the English government or the people composing it cannot be honestly or unselfishly interested in Ireland.

When the *News* rejected the letter, Solanus turned around and mailed it to *The Irish World* in Manhattan, which ran it word for word.

In the late autumn of 1923, Fr. Benno Aichinger made his scheduled and official visit to the house and parish at 113th and Third Avenue. Fr. Benno was the minister of the Capuchin province and was known as "Father Provincial."

Fr. Benno spent some time learning about the progress of pastoral efforts within the parish. It was also his role to inquire after the spiritual and temporal welfare of each friar within the house. He wanted to know about the ministry of each friar and to hear about any problems being experienced.

It's likely that Fr. Benno talked for a while to the superior of Queen of Angels before he asked him to call in Fr. Solanus. By this time, rumors that Fr. Solanus was a "miracle worker" had spread far enough to be heard by the most influential Capuchin ears, and Fr. Benno was concerned about the situation.

It was not Franciscan philosophy to permit any friar to bask in the limelight of excessive popularity, and certainly not as a "miracle man!" But Fr. Benno knew something of Fr. Solanus. He had been briefed about his struggles in the seminary and his ordination as a priest with limited faculties. He had heard that Solanus had accepted all things with great grace.

On November 8, Fr. Solanus was summoned to talk with Father Provincial. Fr. Benno studied the honest blue eyes, the straight features, and the still very youthful face of the priest before him and could see that he had nothing to fear from the attitude of Fr. Solanus. Fr. Solanus spoke of the phenomenal occurrences as "favors" from God. It seemed that he was trying to redirect credit for these "favors" in the proper direction. These "favors" were being granted through the grace of the Seraphic Mass Association, Solanus explained. He also told Fr. Benno that he simply talked with people, enrolled them in the SMA, and then prayed for their intentions.

Finally, Fr. Benno told Fr. Solanus to begin to separately record all the prayer requests of those who came to see him. If and when prayers were answered, Fr. Benno added, Fr. Solanus was to go back and make note of that "favor" near the original entry. Solanus bowed his head in obedience and promised to do all that the Capuchin provincial had ordered.

When Solanus left Fr. Benno, he went to look around the house for a notebook he might use. He knew very well that there would be a need for it quickly. People would come to see him on the following day. Finally, he came across a twelve-by-ten ledger-style notebook with heavy covers. It would do nicely, Solanus told himself. He sat down and thought for a moment about a title.

"Notes about Special Cases." Solanus penned that at the top of his first page and then proceeded to make a short notation about this notebook's newly ordained purpose. "Nov. 8th, 1923," Fr. Solanus wrote. "Today Visitation closed. Father Provincial wishes notes to be made of special favors reported as through the Seraphic Mass Association."

The closed "Visitation" referred to the fact that for that day, the monastery welcomed no visitors and did none of its usual business because of the visit of the provincial. Fr. Solanus had no people to meet and talk with at his front office desk. The whole day was given over to meeting with the provincial and hearing his pastoral advice.

It wasn't long after Fr. Benno made his good-byes and headed for the next Capuchin stop that Solanus had occasion to pick up his pen and his notebook about "Special Cases." The first entry read:

This P.M. Marg. Quinn — who enrolled her neighbor Mr. Maughan against drink and consequent anger on October 26, as also her sister, E. Remy of Philadelphia against severe inflammatory rheumatism, reports wonderful improvement in former and [reception of] letter this A.M. from [her] sister [writing]: "Thank God and the good prayer society, I'm feeling fine."

Underneath his first entry, Solanus jotted, "Thanks be to God!" From November 8 to December 9, 1923, a wide variety of intentions were jotted on the first page of the notebook, representing a good cross-section of human aspirations and complaints.

One woman from Connecticut came to ask Fr. Solanus to pray for a religious vocation for her son. Another mother arrived in tears because her sixteen-year-old daughter had disappeared. A woman came and enrolled her brother, who had had a serious drinking problem for five years. A couple who had been mugged showed up only to receive tender first aid and a prayer for healing from the doorkeeper. A petitioner asked prayers to alleviate a nervous condition, while another asked prayers to relieve a condition that had made her blind in one eye. Squeezed into the margin near the entry about the drinking brother, another "Thanks be to God" appeared. It was dated December 14, five days after the original entry was made. The woman had come to report that her brother had suddenly stopped drinking and that she was "hopeful."

As Christmas 1923 came closer, the briefly worded, abbreviated notations on needs continued to be recorded. More entries carried happy follow-up reports.

A woman dying of pneumonia recovered. She'd been given only a few hours to live. Another woman came back to tell Fr. Solanus that her life-threatening heart condition had cleared up. A woman who had lost her memory eight years earlier regained it, her husband came to tell Fr. Solanus. A New Jersey man hospitalized in an asylum was healed and reported back to work within four months, his family told Solanus.

Men, women, and children, believers and nonbelievers alike — all seemed to be the beneficiaries of Solanus's enrollment in the SMA. There was no rhyme or rhythm to the remarkable reports of favors. "God is good!" "Thank God!" Solanus repeatedly told dumbfounded people when they returned to Queen of Angels to tell of their blessings. There was no mystery to it, he insisted.

It's true that some sick people certainly improved in a way that may have occurred in the normal course of events. But in other cases, the turnaround seemed totally unexplainable from a medical perspective.

In a letter written to Father Provincial in January 1924, Fr. Solanus mentioned the great financial blessings the SMA was bringing to the missions. "Father Guardian just told me that the cash received this month already is $1002.00," he wrote. "Thanks be to God! The report of favors as through this source continue."

In February 1924, a man named Patrick McCue was enrolled in the Seraphic Mass Association by a friend. McCue, a motorman, was in Belleview Hospital, suffering from diabetes and a gangrenous toe. Doctors told him that it was likely that his leg would have to be amputated. McCue's condition took a sudden and complete turn for the better, however, after the SMA enrollment. Surgery was called off; the infection disappeared on its own. By the end of March, Patrick McCue was back at work. Gradually, people came from increasingly distant locations to ask for counsel and prayers from Fr. Solanus. This meant that word of the special ministry was being spread farther afield by those who had already had contact with him.

Whatever the superiors of Fr. Solanus were waiting to see was very soon visible to them. On July 30, he was told that they had decided to move him once again. This time, the move was to be out of New York and back to Detroit. St. Bonaventure's, after all, was headquarters for the order. If the ministry of Fr. Solanus was going to continue to attract crowds of people daily, perhaps it could be better handled in Detroit.

Between November 8, 1923, and July 28, 1924, Solanus had made ninety-six entries about cases in his notebook. Later, it was seen that forty-one of them carried added notations indicating that prayers had been answered. Within two days, Fr. Solanus had dutifully and punctually reported at St. Bonaventure's — by his August 1 deadline. No farewell banquets had been arranged and there'd been little time to wrap up any unfinished commitments to people or projects at Our Lady, Queen of Angels Parish. Solanus knew he would be leaving a part of his heart in New York at Sacred Heart, at Our Lady of Sorrows, and at Queen of Angels.

Years later, Solanus wrote to his brother Jim of his New York leave-taking.

While I never long to go back to any old place from which Divine Providence has seen good to remove me, yet I must acknowledge that I have a natural inclination that way — like the Israelites in the desert naturally yearning (many of them) to go back to Egypt.

With some twinges of that longing inside of him, Fr. Solanus found himself making his way to his assigned room on a hot day in Detroit to unpack. That probably took even less time than it had when he'd arrived at St. Bonaventure's the first time.

That arrival, in 1896, had been a snowy, stormy Christmas Eve. On this warm August day in 1924, Solanus could only look back at that day of entrance and the stinging December cold and wonder. He was astonished — prayerfully astonished — at the ministry into which the Lord had been leading him right from the beginning.

CHAPTER SEVEN

Back at St. Bonaventure's
(1924–1935)

By 1924, DETROIT WAS RAPIDLY becoming "the Motor City," the automobile center of the world. In 1913, Henry Ford had already settled on an assembly-line approach that was to revolutionize automobile production. In the decade following, the future looked bright and exciting for the city. Even the Capuchin monastery on Mt. Elliott Avenue, on the city's east side, was becoming comfortable with a few twentieth-century comforts.

In 1897, the year before Fr. Solanus had moved on to study in Milwaukee, the friars decided to put in electric lights, and soon, the chapel and all the rooms of St. Bonaventure glowed with modern light fixtures. Ten years later, in 1907, a hot-water heating system was installed to heat the chapel when the old system failed. Friars, after all, spent hours in prayer, sitting or kneeling in an otherwise chilly chapel. In 1909, the first telephone was installed, and the Capuchins then had a link to the outside world. During a short talk with the superior of the house, Fr. Solanus discovered that he would again be a sort of human link to that outside world.

His official assignment was to be assistant porter, helping out the friary porter, Br. Francis Spruck. Unofficially, it was

expected that his role of counseling and praying with people would continue. It was thought that Br. Francis needed help, since he was also the tailor for the province. Br. Francis had to cut and sew the habits for men all over the province. To facilitate his dual role, Francis had been given two rooms near the friary's main entrance. The tailor shop was on the right side of the door, with a porter's office on the other.

Posing for the photographer at the entrance to St. Bonaventure's in Detroit, about 1939: From left, Fr. Alphonse Heckler (porter), Br. Francis Spruck (tailor), and Fr. Solanus (assistant porter).

By the early autumn of 1924, however, Br. Francis and Fr. Solanus both saw that the visitor lines at St. Bonaventure were getting longer as the days went by. Most of the visitors, it seemed, wanted to meet or talk with Fr. Solanus.

The guardian, Fr. Innocent Ferstler, and others who heard about the work Fr. Solanus had done in New York, were not surprised by the lines. And Solanus Casey certainly could not have been surprised. He had become very familiar with the powerful needs of spirit and body among all God's people. Those needs were just as common in Detroit as in Manhattan and Yonkers.

Br. Francis Spruck, however, was at first shocked and later distressed by the long lines of petitioners winding their way around the friary's front hall. His job as main porter had once been a manageable one. Now that he had an "assistant," the "routine" portering tasks were getting more and more demanding. There was a crowd in the place every day, and his "assistant" was creating *more* work for him!

Neither could Francis understand why Solanus spent so much time talking with each person. As the doorbell began to ring more and more frequently, Br. Francis found himself having to leave his tailoring table to answer it. Fr. Solanus, he noticed, was almost always too preoccupied in a conversation to answer the door. Visitors told Br. Francis that they wanted to see Solanus, that they had heard that his prayers were so often answered.

Francis would nod politely, but it seemed to him that a scheduled limit of time spent with each person would be more efficient. Fr. Solanus listened to that suggestion very attentively, but never seemed to act upon it. Instead, chairs were set up along the walls; waiting to see him became a bit less tiring, but no less time-consuming.

In one way, the front-door phenomenon surrounding Fr. Solanus was more disruptive for St. Bonaventure's than in the parishes where he'd been assigned. When it was founded in 1883, restrictions had been imposed on the scheduling of High Masses and sermons by the archdiocese, and St. Bonaventure's had been deliberately planned with no parish attached to the monastery to prevent it from drawing people away from parishes. The Capuchins could not have been happier about the "restraints." At this monastery, they wanted the chance for quiet prayer, and the methodical, monastic way of life provided it.

Though Br. Francis had little sympathy for him, Solanus did attempt to blend his day at the porter's desk with the routine prayer life in the monastery. When the community rose for the day at 4:45 A.M., Fr. Solanus was often already up, praying in the chapel. Following night prayer, the other Capuchins were in bed by 9:30 P.M. — but all too frequently at that hour, the assistant porter was still talking to a visitor or two at his desk at the front entrance. It was a wearying pace for anyone, and by now Solanus Casey was in his fifties.

Frequently, Br. Francis would scold Solanus in front of waiting people, calling him simply "Solanus!" when he was irritated. Francis would then announce that people could also come to him for enrollment in the Seraphic Mass Association. Fr. Solanus would meekly nod his head and agree, but no one would leave his seat. People preferred to wait for Fr. Solanus, even if it took twice as long. And it frequently did.

"I have plenty to keep myself busy for at least eighteen hours a day," he wrote, many years later, to his sister Margaret. But by then, the eighteen-hour workday had been part of his life for dozens of years.

In New York, Solanus had made many friends. In Detroit, the same sort of enduring relationships began to develop very soon after he arrived. In January 1925, Solanus met Earl Eagen, a thirty-nine-year-old husband and father from Port Huron, Michigan. Eagen was in pain and in a state of hopelessness with stomach cancer. The man was so low that Solanus later said he'd judged Earl to be seventy-five years old or older. Eagen told the porter that he didn't know who would care for his children.

Following a pattern that had begun in New York, Fr. Solanus asked Earl Eagen and his wife if he could enroll them in the Seraphic Mass Association. The Eagens readily agreed

In this photo, taken about 1939, a visitor watches intently as Fr. Solanus enrolls her in the Seraphic Mass Association at the large oak desk he used near the main entrance of St. Bonaventure's.

to it and promised to donate money for a "perpetual enrollment" as soon as they could afford it.

Eight days later, a rejuvenated Earl Eagen and his wife drove the sixty miles to Detroit on a Sunday morning. Eagen told Fr. Solanus that the stomach pains were gone and that he felt totally well. He was not at all sure, he told the priest, that he would even bother to have the x-rays done which could confirm the disappearance of the cancer. Solanus, smiling with delight, agreed that the money might be better spent for the SMA. A long friendship with the Eagen family began right then and there.

On February 4, 1925, a couple from a Detroit suburb brought their nine-year-old son to see Fr. Solanus. The boy, John Slyker, had very serious vision problems that puzzled the eye specialists who had seen him. John was experiencing double vision in one eye and had no vision in the other. On the way home from St. Bonaventure, after Fr. Solanus had blessed him and enrolled him in the SMA, John began to read street signs; an "unexplainable" but immediate improvement in his vision had begun.

During the 1920s, however, signs of economic troubles ahead began to surface in Detroit. The auto industry became sluggish, and production slowdowns forced the major companies to cut working hours for most of their employees. Many of the Detroiters whom Solanus knew grew worried.

In March 1925, John McKenna, a Chevrolet employee, came to talk with Solanus. He told his Capuchin friend how worried he was about his ability to support his wife and children. Due to the economic slump, working hours at Chevrolet had been reduced to a handful per day. Then McKenna made a bold suggestion to Fr. Solanus: that the whole company — Chevrolet — be enrolled in the Seraphic Mass Association.

Solanus considered the unusual request. He had enrolled individuals in the SMA. He had enrolled families, too. But he had never thought of enrolling a body of people, such as an entire company. Could a company benefit from the graces ensuing from offered Mass intentions and Capuchin prayers? Fr. Solanus didn't really see why not. So, winking at McKenna, he reached for his pen. The wink said simply that God can answer prayer in any way He wishes.

On that same day, John McKenna later heard, Chevrolet received a very large order for automobiles. Soon after, an order for 45,000 cars was placed, and Chevrolet employees were ordered back to work, and even on overtime at that. As soon as he heard that news, an overjoyed McKenna visited Fr. Solanus to give him the good news. There was no question about the fact that this unique ministry and his demanding schedule set Solanus apart from other friars. Clearly, the service he was involved in followed no other previous Capuchin patterns!

Solanus, for instance, was almost always late for meals. He was reluctant to cut off people who had come to seek his help just because his dinner or supper or breakfast was about to be served. "I think he just about ate the one main meal," said a fellow friar. Br. Francis, who had trouble understanding the Solanus approach, would frequently enter the refectory explaining that Fr. Solanus was "still talking, still talking."

Francis seemed to believe that Solanus was too "loose" in the way he dealt with visitors. More control over the situation through tighter scheduling of personal conferences, he believed, would save the monastery and Solanus much inconvenience.

Some mannerisms and traits in Fr. Solanus also prompted teasing from other friars at St. Bonaventure. But Solanus Casey had been raised in a family of sixteen children, and this kind of thing didn't faze him. He shrugged off the jokes about his high-pitched wispy voice. "Nobody understands you; open your mouth!" he was told. "God understands me," he would comment.

Solanus also had an unusual eating habit: in the morning, at breakfast, he would pour everything he was consuming into one bowl. Coffee and orange juice would slosh around in the bowl with cold or hot cereal. It's likely that it was a sort of self-imposed mortification, but some of his brother Capuchins teased him continually about it. When somewhat sharper remarks came his way about his violin-playing, Solanus seemed to turn a deaf ear to them. It was a matter of give and take. He took the wisecracks and gave his concerts anyway.

With the time he had, Fr. Solanus did make efforts to be as fully involved as possible in community life. He enjoyed people, and when the friars met at recreation time, he liked to participate. On Sunday evenings, he would come into the refectory and pour himself a glass of wine from the gallon jug by holding it over his shoulder. He was clearly ready to mix with others and enjoy himself. He had a natural knack for spinning tales about Ireland, his childhood, or youth. At billiards or pool, he was considered a tough opponent — until his call bell or a phone call would interrupt his game. Then, his brother Capuchins recalled, he would hang up his pool cue and head for his porter's desk. He knew he wouldn't be back quickly.

The visitors continued to come, day after day, month after month. The front door of the monastery, previously always locked, was now open all the time, and Solanus hung a sign outside that said, "Walk in." This eliminated the nuisance of a doorbell ringing constantly.

As the seasons moved on by the Capuchin monastery on Mt. Elliott Avenue, the pattern did not change much. Sitting at his desk, Fr. Solanus continued to enroll hundreds of people in the Seraphic Mass Association. And the "favors" being reported didn't stop.

On January 20, 1927, thirty-year-old Anna Schram was taken from her Detroit home to the hospital for surgery. One month after an operation for gallstones, doctors told her that she had developed an abscess of the liver. They admitted that they did not know of any patient who had survived such an operation. Anna's sister phoned Fr. Solanus at St. Bonaventure and had Anna enrolled. Less than one month after Fr. Solanus had enrolled the young woman in the SMA, her sister told Solanus that Anna was already home and was recovering. Visitors were also recovering from illnesses and complaints following the Wednesday afternoon healing service, held each week at 3:00 P.M. in the chapel. For years, the Capuchins had been offering a blessing called the "St. Maurus Blessing of the Sick." The blessing, with a Benedictine history, had come from a sixth-century monk named Maurus who had a gift of healing.

When Fr. Solanus moved to St. Bonaventure's, the prayer service grew in popularity. But it was a struggle for Solanus himself to get there on time. Right up until the clock struck three o'clock, he would be at his desk, meeting with someone. Finally, Br. Francis would stand directly in front of Solanus and his visitor, tapping his foot and whispering sharply, "Casey!" Then Fr. Solanus would quietly apologize that he had to leave. The two, Francis and Solanus, would walk through a hallway connecting the friary to the chapel. Disappointed people waiting to see and talk with Fr. Solanus either followed him to church to attend the service or waited for his return. At dinner later in the day, Francis frequently scolded Solanus for all of his "idle words." Following a short *ferverino*, or talk, at the healing service, Fr. Solanus would bless those attending with a relic of the True Cross. He was not always assigned to lead the service, but he always wore the same red stole and used the same relic of the True Cross for it. And, when he was scheduled to lead it, people arrived early and sat at the front of the chapel.

Part of the reason for sitting up front was so people could actually hear him. His weak voice frequently made that difficult, but his words almost always touched on trust in God, thanking God, or the virtues of faith and charity. The blessing of St. Maurus was then pronounced for all:

Through the invocation of the most holy name of the Lord, may that faith in which St. Maurus, by employing the words that follow, healed the sick, and in which I, though an unworthy servant, utter the selfsame words, restore your health as you desire. In the name of the most holy and undivided Trinity, and supported by the merits of the most holy Fr. Benedict, I bid you to rise, stand on your feet, and be cured. In the name of the Father, and of the Son, and of the Holy Ghost. Amen.

Near the end of 1928, Fr. Maurice came to visit his brother Solanus at St. Bonaventure's. Maurice was then sixty-one years old and had been a priest for seventeen years. But Fr. Maurice was not settled, and Solanus listened, as he listened to so many people, with great attention. Maurice, it seemed, wanted to become a member of the Capuchin order and leave the diocesan priesthood.

Fr. Solanus knew that his brother had not been happy in his parish ministry in the West, although he couldn't quite understand the reason for it. Nonetheless, he arranged for Maurice to talk to the superiors of the order about becoming a Capuchin. By the end of his visit with his younger brother, Maurice was able to plan to return and enter the Capuchin novitiate during the following year. He left Detroit happy, but Fr. Solanus was troubled.

On Christmas Eve, his worries about Maurice were overshadowed by other sad family news. Ellie — as the eldest of the Casey siblings was called — had died in Seattle, at the age of sixty-four.

The last year of the 1920s began in a very predictable way, as far as the Capuchins of St. Bonaventure's were concerned.

The weather was cold and wet. The lines of visitors coming to talk with Fr. Solanus were filled with people with anxious eyes. And there were phone calls and people at the door in the middle of the night.

"Any time that anyone came to the monastery at night, Fr. Solanus would answer the bell," remembered Fr. Herman Buss, whose room was adjacent to Solanus's. "None of the others were inclined to disturb their rest. I would always hear the 'slop-slop' of his sandals." On January 25, 1929, Fr. Solanus heard the doorbell again and got up. A Western Union delivery man was holding a telegram addressed to him, bearing the unhappy news that his brothers John and Tom had been killed that evening in a car accident near Seattle. John, fifty-nine, and Tom, fifty-four, both lawyers, had been on their way home after trying a case together. Solanus bit his lip with the pain and made his way to the chapel. Three from his family gone in less than a month!

In the spring and summer, hundreds of people continued to make their way to Mt. Elliott Avenue. Some came over from the new Chrysler plant that had been completed nearly a year earlier, in 1928. The plant was to be the last major automobile plant built within the city limits. In July, Fr. Solanus marked the twenty-fifth anniversary of his ordination. Maurice came to help him celebrate the occasion and then prepared to enter the Capuchin novitiate. The order had been receiving so many vocations that a new novitiate building was built in Huntington, Indiana. Frs. Solanus and Maurice headed for the small community, surrounded by farmlands, about twenty-five miles southwest of Fort Wayne.

On September 10, with Fr. Solanus assisting at the ceremony, Maurice was invested as a Capuchin along with a group

of young men. Maurice was to be known in the order as
Fr. Maurice Joachim. Eventually, Maurice was accepted into
the order as a Third Order member only. (The Third Order is
known today as the Secular Franciscan Order.) The Capuchins
were apparently reluctant to permit him to profess vows in the
congregation at the "advanced" age of sixty-two. Solanus concluded that his brother was finally where he should be and,
happy about Maurice's new start, he returned to Detroit.
About six weeks after Fr. Solanus returned, however, the world
fell apart — or so it seemed, to many Detroiters and millions
of other Americans. On October 29, 1929, the Stock Market
crashed. It signaled the beginning of a financial collapse with
no historical parallel. Alfred E. Smith, the Catholic New
Yorker who'd run for president of the United States as a
Democrat the year before, said later that the Great Depression that followed was "equivalent to war."

People in Detroit believed that they were on the front line
of that war. Detroit had become the most important industrial
city in the country by 1930, and thus the disaster probably hit
Detroit harder than any other American city. Motor vehicle
production dropped from 5.3 million annually in 1929 to 1.3
million by 1932. It wasn't long before there were even more
people lined up at the monastery doors on Mt. Elliott Avenue.
But this time, many of them needed something besides prayers
and a willing listener. They needed food.

In fact, it had always been a practice at the monastery to
feed the needy who came to the door, and so the Capuchins
quickly increased the amount of food available for the hungry.
Before the Great Depression really began, about one hundred
people came each day for some coffee, soup, and a slice or two
of bread. Even this became too much for the porters Solanus

and Francis to handle. After the Crash, Fr. Capistran Claude, the superior of the monastery, immediately asked the Third Order of St. Francis to help. The Third Order was a group of lay people linked with Franciscans through the pledge to observe certain religious practices and a Franciscan spirit. Fr. Herman Buss, who directed the Third Order, quickly mobilized the group. On November 2, three days after the Crash, the Third Order opened the doors of a soup kitchen for the first time.

At first, only coffee and rolls were available to the hungry. But, within a few weeks, members of the Third Order began to make a hearty soup which they served at noon. Because of very limited kitchen facilities, they were forced to prepare each day's meal the day before. In the dining room of their hall,

The Capuchin soup kitchen in Detroit, about 1939. Performing the corporal work of "feeding the hungry" are, from left (behind the diners): Frs. Solanus Casy, Salesius Schneweis, Gerard Hesse, Crescentian Volpel, and Matthias Nack. In front of the table is Fr. Theodosius Foley.

rough planks were set up over sawhorses for tables. The hungry, typically men, began to pour in each day. As the Depression cast more and more people into need, the Capuchin soup kitchen was feeding between 1,500 and 3,000 people daily.

Fr. Solanus followed the efforts of the soup kitchen from his desk. At first, he could not become actively involved in the feeding ministry, but his heart was there. When he met people of financial means or influence, he urged them to contribute toward the soup kitchen. Around Christmas time, he met an Irishman named Ray McDonough, who came to help at the soup kitchen after his employer sent him to get involved. Needless to say, Solanus found opportunities for him to help!

Along with a hearty bowl of soup and a beverage, the Capuchins fed the hungry about half a loaf of bread, per person, per meal. Loading up bread on a visitor's tray in this 1942 *Detroit News* photo are, from left: Fr. Matthias Nack, an unidentified Third Order member, and Fr. Solanus Casey.

The new decade, the thirties, opened with a heaviness that few Americans could even describe. The crowds in the waiting room at St. Bonaventure grew larger and larger. Many were men who had lost heart after weeks of joblessness and no means of feeding their families. As the months went by, these men were facing foreclosures on homes or evictions from apartments.

Families were being torn apart, and people correctly suspected that the misery would get worse before it got better. The men at the friary shook their heads in disbelief when it was reported that Henry Ford was calling the Depression "a wholesome thing in general." He mandated that all of his workmen dig vegetable gardens in their backyards or on Ford property or be fired. As a result of these kinds of requirements, many came to St. Bonaventure's sensing that their unemployment and poverty were somehow their own fault. Fr. Solanus disagreed and shared his vision of how God loved them and would watch over them. He also shared the food reserves of the friary pantry — until some of his fellow Capuchins complained!

Fr. Solanus made it his business to make the needs of the kitchen known to the more influential Detroiters he met. Tom Bresnahan, the mayor of River Rouge (a Detroit suburb), began to send help. Later on, Frank Murphy, Detroit's mayor, donated a prize bull he'd won in a raffle.

Even with help, finding enough food to feed as many as 3,000 people each day was difficult for the Capuchins. And it was impossible to predict on a daily basis just how many people would be lining up to eat. An excess of even fifty could run the kitchen out of soup and bread and leave hungry people standing with empty plates. All of the Capuchins agonized when it seemed that there might be a shortage.

Fr. Herman Buss remembered many anxious moments in the kitchen. But one day something happened that he would never forget. He had absolutely no bread to feed a crowd of people already waiting in line. Thinking perhaps that Fr. Solanus could phone one of his more affluent friends, Fr. Herman went over to the monastery and told Solanus of the crisis.

"I said, 'Fr. Solanus, we have no more bread and two or three hundred men are waiting for something to eat.' He went over to the hall and told the men waiting in line, 'Just wait and God will provide.' Fr. Solanus said an 'Our Father' after inviting the men to join him in the prayer. We just turned around and opened the front door to go out, and there was a bakery man coming with a big basket full of food. He had his whole truck full of stuff, and he proceeded to unload it. When the men saw this they started to cry and tears were running down their cheeks. Fr. Solanus, in his simple way, said, 'See, God provides. Nobody will starve as long as you put your confidence in God, in Divine Providence.'"

In 1931 and 1932, the Capuchins started to contact Detroit bakeries to ask for donations of day-old bread. And butchers, hearing about the soup kitchen, gave meat bones for the stockpots. The community as a whole was doing what it could to help its own, to extend a helping hand to those in need.

Still, by early 1933, when Franklin Roosevelt was just beginning his first term as President, an estimated twelve million Americans were out of work. There was little or no money for doctor bills, and illness became even more frightening.

In 1934, the Houlihans' newborn son was exposed to whooping cough. When the tiny baby began to cough, the parents took him to the doctor, who gave him a shot. But the coughing continued.

"We took him at once to Fr. Solanus," Mrs. Houlihan recalled. "As we entered the office, Fr. Solanus was speaking to someone else — but he looked up at us as we waited our turn. Fr. Solanus heard our baby son cough and choke up. Fr. Solanus left his desk and came right over to us and asked what was the trouble with our small baby. Fr. Solanus blessed the baby and told us not to worry, that our son would be all right."

The baby did recover — although the Houlihans' doctor, a Catholic, frankly admitted that he had expected the child to die. "The doctor told us that we were very fortunate to keep our son."

With William Tremblay, who often acted as a driver, Solanus went out to those too sick to come to St. Bonaventure. Many of those he visited were Canadian, since the Canadian border was mere miles outside Detroit. Tremblay remembered a visit to a dying woman, Mrs. Eva Dugall, in Windsor. The woman had tuberculosis and had been on the verge of dying for months, Tremblay said. Anxiety concerning the welfare of her small children kept her alive.

"Father went inside and I went along, too. When he came in, the first thing this lady said was, 'Oh, you look just like Jesus Christ Himself.' Everybody in the room began to cry. 'Well, I'm taking His place,' he said. 'I was sent here by Him. I came because the Lord has a crown waiting for you. Why don't you resign yourself to go to Heaven and forget about your children? The Lord has a lot of good mothers, especially the Blessed Virgin, and she will take care of your children.'"

The woman became peaceful, Tremblay said. Everyone began to pray after Fr. Solanus suggested they say a decade of the Rosary. Then Solanus and his driver left. At 11:00 P.M. that evening, Tremblay later heard, the woman died, leaving her pain behind.

Confidence in God. If any phrase summed up the vision of life of this Capuchin, that was it. But Solanus was not under the impression that confidence in God meant inaction on the part of those in need. He was country-bred. When there was something he could do, he rolled up his sleeves — figuratively and literally — to do it.

One of the burdens of maintaining an adequate food supply, in fact, was a blessing to Fr. Solanus. It was necessary to go out to area farms and pick fruit or vegetables, and Solanus loved to go out in a truck with Ray McDonough, who had become the director of the Capuchin soup kitchen. McDonough would drive, and Fr. Solanus would feast his eyes on fields and farms. Somewhere along the trip, the two would say a Rosary for the poor and for the success of their venture.

"Fr. Solanus accompanied Ray Garland with a truck on a begging trip near Ruth [Michigan]," the chronicle of St. Bonaventure reported on October 25, 1934. "They returned with a load of apples, potatoes, and other vegetables at 2 A.M." Another note entered a month later reported Solanus out again in the Ruth area with Br. Paschal collecting fifty bushels of potatoes, thirty bags of beans, and other foodstuffs.

Still, the deepening of the Great Depression throughout the 1930s stretched everyone's reserves to the limits. And the ministry of Fr. Solanus must have also been taxed. As the expectations of others increased, so did his prayer life. He could not help thinking of the people who came to see him and of their problems. Fatigue and the tedium of his routine were often overwhelming, he admitted later. By nature, he was not a workaholic. Both as a boy and later in life, he enjoyed leisure very much, but it was rapidly disappearing from his life.

Detroit people began to talk of a sort of "knowledge" in Solanus. He always told troubled visitors to pray with faith, but his assurance about events often seemed to go beyond "believing" to become "knowing." He seemed to have an inner prophetic sense about the outcome of many events.

In 1933, according to Mrs. Mary Therese McHugh, her two-year-old daughter became very ill and developed a 104-degree fever. The doctor told Mrs. McHugh that it was a life-threatening situation, but soon the child's fever went even higher. There seemed to be little chance to save her life. Mrs. McHugh's pastor suggested that she call Fr. Solanus at St. Bonaventure's. Solanus told her to bring the child over to him immediately.

Mrs. McHugh wrapped up the child and drove over to the monastery. Fr. Solanus took the little girl into his own arms and prayed silently for a few moments. Then, he returned the child to her mother and told her to come back with the child on Saturday — three days later.

"I told him that the doctors did not expect her to live until Saturday," Mrs. McHugh said later.

"Just do as I wish. Bring her to me; she'll be ready," Fr. Solanus responded.

For Fr. Solanus, there was no question about the outcome for this child. He seemed to be convinced that she would not only recover but would be well enough to leave the house within three days.

That night, as Mrs. McHugh recalled years later, her little girl's fever broke and she began to recover. In the morning, little Marianne woke up and asked for something to eat. The

McHughs' doctor viewed the child's recovery as "a miracle" —
and it was a miracle that Fr. Solanus could apparently see
coming.

Many of the miracles that seemed to touch Fr. Solanus
most personally had to do with conversions — healings of both
the heart and the spirit. Sometimes, such feelings changed the
direction of the person's life dramatically . . . and humorously.
Solanus reported on one such conversion to his good friend
William Tremblay years later.

Early one morning during these early 1930s, around four
o'clock, Solanus got up to answer the doorbell at the front entrance. He was one of the monastery porters, after all. A man
who'd obviously been drinking stood waiting for him on the
step. "Where's that guy Solanus?" the man wanted to know,
slurring his words a bit.

"Well, he's here. What do you want with him?" Solanus
answered.

"I came here to kill him," the man replied.

"Well," Solanus said, "that's something that should be discussed."

The porter then invited this would-be murderer into the
monastery and sat him down on the other side of his desk. In
a few moments, the man spilled out the reasons for his desire
to kill a priest he'd never met. He was a Communist, he told
Fr. Solanus, but his mother was a devoted Catholic and was a
friend of this Fr. Solanus. She cried all the time about her son's
Communist views and his abandonment of the Church. The
man was tired of her interference and even more tired of hearing about Solanus.

Solanus listened patiently. He nodded appreciatively and
even smiled a bit. When the fellow was all talked out and

sobered just a little, Fr. Solanus began to talk. He talked about the Church, about God's mercy, and about the godlessness of Communism. By the time Fr. Solanus was finished, the man's heart was completely changed. He wanted to go to confession. Besides the fact that he was not permitted to hear anyone's confession, Solanus wanted the man to receive the blessings of Penance when he was completely sober. So he told the man that he should come back later in the light of day to do that. When the man left, Solanus shut off the lights and headed for the chapel. The monastery day started at 4:45 A.M., anyway.

CHAPTER EIGHT

Longer Lines and Longer Hours
(1935–1945)

ON MAY 16, 1935, the chronicler at St. Bonaventure Monastery had a rather strange incident to record about the assistant porter, Fr. Solanus Casey. He wrote:

> Fr. Solanus to his great joy recovered his Mass Association Record book. He had misplaced it a few days ago but could not recall where he had put it. He went to the Post Office and found it there.

The chronicler goes on to explain the probable sequence of events: Fr. Solanus had placed his record book with a bundle of letters he had just picked up at the post office. On the way out, without thinking he dropped the bundle of mail — along with his Seraphic Mass Association ledger — in a mailbox. Postal employees, later discovering the letters and ledger, contacted a grateful Fr. Solanus.

Since he had come to Detroit to the Capuchin provincialate eleven years earlier, Solanus Casey had been living at a pace that would have finished many sixty-four-year-old men.

As a result, he had little time and little mental energy left to sort things — let alone information — into the proper "incoming" and "outgoing" categories. Life was hectic, and only the peace of prayer and the Blessed Sacrament in the chapel seemed to make it tolerable.

Throughout the summer of 1935, Solanus was also serving on weekend "help-outs" at Detroit parishes. Generally, this meant saying several Masses, and then returning to the friary. He was at the friary on the day Br. André Bessette of Montreal stopped to visit him. Br. André, a French Canadian Holy Cross brother, was then ninety. Like Solanus, he had also been a porter and had become famous in Canada. Thousands claimed healing through his prayers and special devotion to St. Joseph.

When they met, Br. André asked Fr. Solanus for his blessing. It was given. Fr. Solanus in turn asked for, and received, the aged brother's blessing. Then, the two parted. It was a brief meeting, for Fr. Solanus spoke no French and Br. André did not speak English. But perhaps the calling of God's blessing upon each other said everything they needed to say to each other.

On November 25, Solanus turned sixty-five. This birthday may not have seemed any different from other birthdays. There was no thought of his retirement — either in his mind or in the minds of his superiors at St. Bonaventure's Monastery. His beard was totally gray now and there was very little hair on the top of his head. His oldest brother, Jim, the oldest surviving sibling, had reached his seventieth birthday.

It was a considerable consolation for Solanus that Jim and his other brothers and sisters were doing well and were relatively healthy. The Casey clan was prospering. A good, healthy crop of fourth-generation Caseys — grandchildren of his brothers and sisters — was being born and growing up, mostly in the Far West.

He fondly recalled the parishes and friends he'd come to know in New York, but Solanus seemed to be in the right place at St. Bonaventure's. Detroit was sure of it. In one of the most difficult eras of its history, during these years of the Great Depression, he had become something of a local celebrity.

The reputation of Fr. Solanus had its predictable result as the 1930s moved along: more and more people came to St. Bonaventure's to see him. The reasons for their visits were no different than the visits of hundreds who had come before: failing eyesight, terminal diseases, marital difficulties, dying children, joblessness, anxiety, depression, the desire for a spiritual conversion of a husband, wife, brother, son. Though the names and faces were different, the stories must have seemed very familiar to Fr. Solanus month after month, year after year.

Many doctors in the Motor City were also hearing of the priest who seemed to have a connection with miraculous healings. After Fr. Solanus prayed for sick individuals, some went back to their physicians later, and more than one doctor could offer no explanation for a sudden cessation of a disease or for the apparent overnight healing of bones or injured tissue or muscles. One of the Capuchin guardians, Fr. Marion Roessler, recalled a hospital's offer of records to substantiate "healing" claims:

> I recall on one occasion that we received word from a Catholic hospital in Detroit, that their authorities would willingly furnish the medical history and x-ray plates of some cases which were suddenly cured after the patients had received the assurance of Fr. Solanus's prayers, his bless-

ing, and/or his enrolling them in the Seraphic Mass Association. However, I no longer remember the name of that hospital.

Fr. Marion Roessler was clearer about the details of a healing he himself saw during these years:

It was the cure of a crippled child who had not walked in
years. She was held in the lap of an adult, sitting at some
distance from Fr. Solanus's desk. Fr. Solanus enrolled the
child in the Seraphic Mass Association, and blessed her.
Then he told her to walk over to him. She immediately got to
her feet and walked, going straight to his desk. The youngster's parents were almost hysterical with joy.

When healings occurred instantly, tears would well up in
Solanus's blue eyes. Witnessing the goodness of God under-
standably moved him.

While Fr. Solanus placed his greatest trust in God as
healer, he never rejected the need for medical doctors. He frequently suggested that people go to doctors to identify ailments or to seek continuing treatment for a health problem.
And yet, he also advised that doctors would not be helpful in
certain cases, or that they simply were not needed. This sort of
counsel, of course, proved controversial — even though there
never was an example of damaging advice from Solanus with
respect to medical care. The foreknowledge that the porter
seemed to have was as awesome as the gift of healing working
through him. And reports of this ability to foresee events were
circulating more frequently in Detroit in the thirties.

"God will take care of it for you," he would tell hundreds of people, who would then see healings or resolved problems. Solanus, it seems, could even see when one patient would improve and when another would be dying. In 1935, this gift of prophecy was demonstrated in a visit one day to two patients at St. Joseph Mercy Hospital.

Fr. Solanus had been phoned and asked to visit a Sister Mary Joseph. She was desperately ill with a severe streptococcus infection on the right side of her throat. Her fever had risen to 105 degrees and her neck had gone rigid. She was slipping into a coma while suffering choking spells. Antibiotics such as penicillin and Terramycin (a brand name for oxytetracycline) were not yet in use. The doctors had told the hospital supervisor, a nun, that they feared the worst for Sister Mary Joseph.

When Fr. Solanus arrived, he went to the sick nun's bedside and began to read about Christ's Passion in the Gospels. Though Sister Mary Joseph had been coughing when he began, the choking spell soon passed. Solanus also blessed her with the relic of the True Cross that he used during Wednesday healing services. After two hours of reading and prayer, he told the nuns assembled around Sister Mary Joseph's hospital bed that she would recover and join them soon.

On the way out of the hospital, however, a man stopped Fr. Solanus in the hallway. His wife had just had minor surgery, he told the priest. Then he asked the Capuchin if he would stop at her room for a moment just to bless her. Fr. Solanus did so. But as he left the woman's room, the priest put his hand on the husband's arm and told him that his wife would soon die.

Solanus gently asked the shocked man to give his wife back to her Creator, then quietly turned and headed for a car with the hospital chauffeur who was to drive him back to St. Bonaventure. Later, the driver learned that the man's wife had died a short time after they had walked out of the hospital.

In 1936, Fr. Solanus was involved in the reconciliation of a husband and wife when a bitter separation and divorce seemed inevitable. William Tremblay remembered the situation because these people were friends. The husband had confessed to him one day that he'd been having an affair but wanted to break it off. The "other woman," however, threatened to expose him to his wife if he abandoned the illicit relationship. Tremblay told his friend to tell his wife about it and then took the two to see his other friend Solanus. Fr. Solanus had been briefed about the situation before the three arrived.

After Tremblay walked in with the couple and introduced them to Fr. Solanus, he turned around to leave them with the priest. "Oh, no," Fr. Solanus told Tremblay, "you stay right here. You went through all that trouble and you might have a good idea." And so, Tremblay, feeling fairly embarrassed, stayed for the confrontation.

"They were both crying and angry, especially her," Tremblay reported. "She didn't even want to look at him. So Fr. Solanus told him to tell his story. 'I don't want you to leave anything out. Say everything.'" When the husband began to tell the whole story, his wife wept harder and harder until it was all over.

Then, according to Tremblay, Solanus turned to the wife and urged her to forgive her husband, saying, "Well, that isn't so bad, the man is repentant. The Lord forgave Mary Magdalene, and you have three lovely children outside waiting for the father and mother to get together again." Solanus urged the woman to get up, kiss her husband, and forgive him. She did, and according to Tremblay, their marriage not only survived, it prospered.

In 1936 or 1937, a Detroit woman, Agnes Juergens, developed a terrible pain in her right wrist. Her family physician referred her to a bone specialist. X-ray films revealed a large, web-structured tumor spreading throughout the bones. Trying to remove the tumor, the authorities maintained, would cause the tumor to spread. They advised the patient, a wife and mother, that they would have to amputate her arm at the elbow.

"When the doctor said that they would have to amputate, we went to see Fr. Solanus," Mrs. Juergens said, more than twenty years later. "Fr. Solanus took my hand, held the wrist, and his eyes were closed. He was praying like he saw a vision or something. When he opened his eyes, he said, 'No, we're not going to let them amputate.' I could just feel that he was seeing something like a vision, that he could see that I would not have to have that operation. After that was when the change began."

"The change" was a halt to the tumor growth. Doctors later verified it, and three months of treatments apparently dissolved the tumor. "They did not have to amputate," Mrs. Juergens said. "They were so amazed that my arm was saved."

Healings reported through Fr. Solanus touched bodies, spirits, relationships — and sometimes, all three. In 1936, a suburban Detroit resident named Mrs. Martin Wachinger began to take a woman to the Wednesday healing services. This woman was a relative who suffered terrible trauma as a result of brain surgery. During the surgery, a physician told Mrs. Wachinger, an optical nerve had been severed. The woman was rendered blind and mentally incompetent, and wasn't expected to survive long.

After about six months of attendance at the Wednesday services, Mrs. Wachinger noticed that the woman's general health seemed to improve. Finally, eyesight returned to one eye and then to the other. Later still, she began to speak and recover mental faculties. Four years later, the woman whom doctors had given up on had recovered so much that she enrolled in a secretarial course. After obtaining a job, the woman got married and kept her own house. Throughout it all, she lived in good health and in happiness once seen as "impossible."

In October 1936, Fr. Solanus learned that his younger brother Leo, only fifty-eight, had died in Seattle. With the death of Leo, three of his nine brothers were gone. Solanus always longed to be closer to his family, but on certain occasions the desire sometimes grew keener.

Despite the long days, there was still time for Solanus to write to his brothers and sisters across the country. The time may have come out of hours that could more reasonably be used for sleeping. However, Solanus saw it as time well spent. He was very attached to his family. Some of his long letters were by now going out of the country. In the 1930s, Solanus's brother Msgr. Edward, nine years his junior, had left his teaching post at St. Thomas College in St. Paul, Minnesota, to become a missionary in the Philippines.

In 1936, Fr. Maurice Joachim Casey, then sixty-nine, began to confide in Solanus his deep and growing disappointment with a few Capuchin superiors who had been cautious about a background of instability in him. Maurice was to live with Capuchin friars but was only under the authority of the house superior where he was living. He was also free to keep his own money, since he had not taken the vow of poverty. But even with his freedom, Fr. Maurice Joachim was becoming increasingly distressed and depressed.

In the summer of 1936, Solanus went to New York to see Maurice. His brother was assigned to parish work at Our Lady of Sorrows Parish in Manhattan. Fr. Maurice was also celebrating the twenty-fifth anniversary of his ordination in June. Our Lady of Sorrows was familiar ground for Solanus. This parish had been his second assignment, and a very unique one. Those three years represented a time of great spiritual peace and growth for him. When Fr. Solanus arrived, he discovered how troubled his older brother was becoming in that same house. Maurice was disgruntled because his superiors did not wish to adopt a plan he had developed for promoting prayer. Solanus noticed that Maurice had made many friends and was doing well pastorally in Manhattan. But in the eyes of Fr. Maurice Joachim, the painful parts of life were overshadowing the joys and successes.

Some months later, Fr. Solanus greeted a letter received from Maurice with great enthusiasm. St. Joseph Church at Prescott, Wisconsin, near the first Casey homestead, was celebrating its seventy-fifth jubilee in the summer of 1937. Maurice had asked Fr. Solanus if he could break away from St. Bonaventure's for a week to go with him to the celebration. Maurice also explained that he also asked Msgr. Ed if he could come for it from the Philippines. It would be time they could all spend together.

Fr. Solanus needed no coaxing to consider the idea. He believed that it would be good to spend time with his brothers — brothers by blood and brothers in ordination. And he knew that the experience might be of special benefit in helping Maurice to forget his heartaches for awhile. Solanus found a few minutes late one evening to write to Ed, urging him to return from the Philippines for the trip if he could.

And so, the three Caseys met in Chicago one summer day and headed for western Wisconsin. Fr. Solanus wore a black suit with Roman collar for the first time. The Capuchin rule had been changed, and he thought it would be more comfortable for travel than the Capuchin habit, but he felt strange in the suit. Later, he asked Maurice and Ed if his beard, spread down over his chest and over his collar, made him look more like a Jewish rabbi than a Roman Catholic priest. The three chuckled over that.

At Trimbelle, the brothers toured the parish where they had received religious training and where Msgr. Edward Casey had been baptized. The three then met up with eighty-three year-old Alex Hupert, who'd bought the Casey farm from Bernard Casey Sr. when the family moved on to Burkhardt, Wisconsin, in 1882. Overjoyed to see the Casey sons now priests, Alex invited them to come out to have dinner and to see the place again the next day. Msgr. Edward joked that he would love to, in return for the nostalgic joy of pitching bundles of hay — a job he'd done often as a young man. Solanus laughed and said that he simply wanted to walk the farm he'd lived on as a boy.

On the day of the visit, Solanus, Maurice, and Edward stopped to visit the graves of their little sisters, Mary Ann and Martha. It was the first time that Solanus and Edward had ever visited their graves. Edward was born after their deaths and Solanus had been very sick with diphtheria himself when both little girls had died.

Solanus found the place familiar, but different. He saw the area where the Caseys had often seen deer moving past bushes along a ravine. Now, the bushes were dwarfed by trees, and the fields were so overgrown that he could no longer see the hill he'd climbed often. On another hill overlooking the spring was the shell of the cabin the Caseys had once fondly called their "new house." Only the cellar was left. A thirty-foot oak had also grown up right in the middle of where the cabin once stood.

But other aspects of the trip brought unexpected joys: as they drove through the farmlands and valleys, trying to identify places they hadn't seen in decades, Fr. Solanus also met priests who had studied with him at St. Francis' diocesan seminary in the 1890s.

The entire adventure of this "return to roots" was later retold for brothers and sisters in a long letter Solanus wrote. Seventeen pages in length, it was like a diary account of this late summer excursion. Solanus wanted to share the joys of the trip with his entire family, but it was sent, first of all, to his oldest brother, Jim. At the time, Jim was sick. Solanus did the next best thing he could do to taking Jim along.

It was also in 1937 that Fr. Solanus was asked to deliver a five-minute talk on a Detroit radio station. The city saw that the worst years of the Great Depression were over. It seemed to be a good time to say "thank you" to the Capuchins for their lifesaving charity to the needy. Though Fr. Solanus was still only the monastery porter and certainly did not have a resonant voice, there seemed to be no better spokesman for the Capuchins of the city. Solanus himself had great respect for the medium of radio. He was a friend and admirer of Fr. Charles Coughlin, the "radio priest" from nearby Royal Oak, who was very popular then.

The radio talk by Fr. Solanus had no political message that would have reminded his listeners of Fr. Coughlin. It was set up in conjunction with an appreciation program put on by the cities of Detroit and Windsor, Ontario, across the Detroit River in Canada. It wasn't a surprise to those who knew him

While he often helped to feed others, Fr. Solanus (second from left) was occasionally a very welcome guest at parish and Catholic organization dinners. This photo, taken at one of them, probably dates from the 1940s.

that Fr. Solanus used this occasion honoring the Capuchins to thank others outside the order.

He thanked the bakers who'd donated bread, the farmers who'd given vegetables, and the butchers who'd supplied meat bones for those hundreds of pots of soup. Solanus also thanked the many benefactors who'd donated funds to help subsidize the Capuchin soup kitchen. It was a simple talk, and Detroit people listening to the high-pitched voice of Solanus must have smiled. Solanus rarely accepted thanks for what he gave. Passing along the praise for good works was utterly consistent with the man's style and spirituality.

Meanwhile, Solanus was much less sure about what to say to his own brother Fr. Maurice Joachim. Having been transferred by the Capuchins to the order's seminary at Marathon, Wisconsin, in 1937, Maurice had grown more dissatisfied with Capuchin life. Throughout that year and 1938, he was considering leaving the order to return to the diocesan priesthood. Fr. Solanus was kind but blunt about his views of such an attempt. Solanus wrote him that the diocese which Maurice had left to become a Capuchin could hardly be expected to welcome back a seventy-one-year-old priest who was unhappy. But Fr. Maurice Joachim was beyond listening to such counsel. Emotionally disturbed, he could no longer hear his brother, a man so many people took great pains to consult. One day in 1938, the pastor of St. Paul's Maltese Parish, Fr. Michael Z. Cefai, was sitting in the provincial superior's office at St. Bonaventure. Fr. Cefai had just been explaining his need for a priest to help with Masses at his parish on the weekends. Fr. Marion Roessler, the superior, had been looking over the list of men still available to assign for weekend duty. It didn't look encouraging, Fr. Cefai said years later.

Then Fr. Marion admitted that he had a few older priests left, including Fr. Solanus Casey; but Fr. Solanus wasn't "allowed to go out, does not hear confessions, and can't speak Maltese."

At just that moment, Fr. Solanus happened to come into the office on another matter, Fr. Cefai recalled. When told of the reason for Fr. Cefai's visit, Fr. Solanus immediately volunteered for weekend help at St. Paul's, if Fr. Marion approved. And so Fr. Solanus began to go to St. Paul's each weekend to say Mass. He continued to do so every week until 1942, and occasionally until 1945. Doing so added to the strain on him. Very quickly, people flocked to him at the parish in the same way that they descended upon St. Bonaventure's. Finding it hard to say no, Fr.

Solanus, with the permission of Frs. Cefai and Marion, began to stay after the Masses to counsel people. Hundreds came to St. Paul's to see him during those hours when he was theoretically free of the task back home at St. Bonaventure's.

From all that he heard and saw, Fr. Solanus was deeply disappointed with the Roosevelt administration. "I say God bless him, too," Solanus wrote to his sister Margaret, "though my enthusiasm for him is almost, or fast becoming ancient history." In his eyes, little seemed to be done for the poor and the hungry. The lines at the soup kitchen were just as long or longer in 1937 as they had been in 1929. Detroit's picture seemed to be no better. Automobile production, the city's "bread and butter," did not recover its 1929 levels until 1948.

Throughout 1937 and 1938, Fr. Solanus felt a need to consult with his brother Msgr. Edward. Edward had stayed on in the United States after the trip to western Wisconsin. He was commissioned to raise funds for the Philippine missions. But his travels left him free to visit his brother Solanus from time to time. The two discussed Maurice and how they might help him.

For his part, Fr. Maurice was by then suffering physically as well as psychologically. A painful carbuncle, or boil, on the back of his neck was giving him some trouble. Doctors in Marathon did not know how to treat it. When the Capuchin superiors sent Maurice to clinics in the Fond du Lac area, the results were no more encouraging.

Fr. Maurice Joachim apparently became disgusted with his Capuchin community when they couldn't find help for him. Perhaps he was also offended that his own brother, Solanus, so well known for his gift of healing, could not or would not help him. In any case, Maurice left his Capuchin residence at

Marathon and went to visit Fr. Charles Coughlin in Royal Oak, a Detroit suburb. There seemed to be no plan for his life, other than to "leave the Capuchins."

Only when Fr. Coughlin urged Maurice to call Solanus did Fr. Solanus learn that his older brother was nearby. Solanus talked with him and agreed to arrange a meeting between Maurice and the provincial. The meeting took place and Maurice received what he wanted — a letter of exit from the Capuchins.

Just what effect all of this had on Fr. Solanus can only be imagined. He surely talked with Msgr. Edward about the whole situation prior to Ed's return to the missions. But seeing Fr. Maurice Joachim searching aimlessly for fulfillment in his priesthood was surely painful to his family. Yet it may have been more difficult for Fr. Solanus than for any of the other Caseys. It was Solanus's example that had inspired Maurice to try the seminary a second time. And it was to the Capuchins, the order Solanus chose, that Maurice had once been drawn.

Nonetheless, there was little that anyone could do to guide Maurice or to console his worried family. For a while, they weren't sure even where Maurice was. Finally, Solanus was informed that Maurice was at the Mt. Hope Sanitarium in Baltimore. During the summer of 1940, the Molloy family of Detroit drove Solanus east to visit Maurice. For two weeks, the brothers spent time together.

Solanus may have needed the trip away as much as Maurice needed to see his brother. In the spring of 1940, the assistant porter had been sick for weeks with colds and flu made more persistent probably by fatigue. In the world at large, there was little news that would have given peace of mind to seventy-two-year-old Fr. Maurice in Baltimore. In Europe, British and

French troops were already at war with Germany. As did other Americans, the Capuchins followed the grim chain of global events. As Franciscans committed to peace, the men at St. Bonaventure Monastery renewed and redoubled their commitments to prayer. The electricity bill for lights in the chapel edged up as the threat of war increased.

In the autumn of 1939, Germany had invaded Poland, a country that had alliances with Great Britain and France. As President Franklin D. Roosevelt watched the progress of war over the preceding twelve months, he became privately convinced that the United States could not remain neutral indefinitely. Publicly, however, he swore that his presidency would not send American men onto battlefields. Right after his third election in 1940, however, President Roosevelt said that the United States would supply war *materiel* to nations at war with Germany and Italy. Everyone knew that this would involve the United States in the war sooner or later.

On Sunday, December 7, 1941, the Capuchins at St. Bonaventure heard about the surprise attack by Japan at Pearl Harbor in Hawaii. The Japanese had attacked at 7:55 A.M., a time when the warships were in the harbor and planes were on the ground. Twenty-three hundred American servicemen were killed in the bombing and strafing. President Roosevelt went to a joint session of Congress the next day and asked for a declaration of war against Japan.

December 8 was also the Feast of the Immaculate Conception. For almost a century under that title, Mary had been patroness of the United States. The Capuchins and many others saw the feast day "declaration of war" as a sign that the United States should seek the special protection of Mary as it entered World War II.

With the coming of war, the Great Depression came to an end. The economy became a wartime economy as factories were adapted to produce war goods. Detroit went back to work making jeeps, trucks, and tanks while hundreds of the city's men went to war. At St. Bonaventure's, the soup lines began to get shorter, although the Capuchins never did close the soup kitchen they'd opened in 1929.

While the rhythm of life was radically altered by war in almost every part of the world, the life of prayer at St. Bonaventure remained the same. Though his working hours were longer, the routine for Fr. Solanus Casey was not very different than it had been twenty years earlier.

One day, Solanus was visited by Steve Gergely of Detroit. The panic-stricken man begged Fr. Solanus to go to the hospital and bless his wife, Leona, who was near death. She had contracted pneumonia after sur-

Although Fr. Solanus disliked "celebrity" status, he was occasionally persuaded to sit for formal photographs. This is a portrait taken c. 1940, showing him with his Bible.

gery. Fr. Solanus could not go. He was on his way to say Mass, but he took off a medal of St. Theresa and told Steve to pin it on Leona. The nurses and Mr. Gergely saw a change for the better immediately. Not every request got such undivided attention, however. During this period, one woman from Detroit called Fr. Solanus on the phone often. The friary phone was near his desk and answering it was part of his responsibilities as porter.

One day, Solanus took the call, listened to the woman, made a few comments, and then hooked the receiver on the wooden shelf just above his desk. Then he proceeded to talk with the visitor on the other side of his desk. Every few minutes or so, he would take the phone, listen, make a remark, and put the receiver down again. After a while, he noticed that everyone was observing this charade. After he picked up the phone the next time, he grinned and silently mouthed the words *she's still talking*!

People came and left St. Bonaventure's Monastery on Mt. Elliott Avenue in astounding numbers. Sometime in 1940, Mrs. Martha Casey, the wife of Solanus's brother Owen, stopped to visit at St. Bonaventure. Solanus had never met the lady and took time to entertain her until he had to return to his desk. A young Capuchin brother came in to talk with Mrs. Casey instead. After a while, Martha asked the brother how many people came to see Fr. Solanus on an average day.

The brother guessed that Fr. Solanus typically saw between one hundred fifty to two hundred people each day at St. Bonaventure's. Most of them came simply to ask him for a blessing — a momentary visit. But from forty to fifty others came to talk with him at some length about a problem, illness, or grief. As the wartime draft took more and more men to war, those who had loved ones in the armed forces came to ask prayers for their men.

In June 1941, a Detroit man named Luke Leonard showed up to talk with Solanus. Leonard was well known in the city's real estate circles, but he was fighting a war that never had coverage in any newspaper. Leonard was battling alcoholism and was losing the battle. He had tried to taper off but wasn't able to wean himself from the bottle. Finally, on a Sunday morning after having had no alcohol for several days, the man walked over to St. Bonaventure's. He was feeling desperately ill and was shaking all over.

Fr. Solanus apparently recognized immediately that Leonard's need for help was urgent. The porter finished talking with a couple and then approached Leonard, who told him that he wanted to talk privately. Inside a private room, Solanus asked when Luke Leonard had recovered from his "illness." The word "illness" and the priest's attitude of quiet encouragement impressed Leonard. He also noticed that Fr. Solanus seemed to believe that the "illness" was already over, that the battle was won.

"You mean my drunk, Father?" Leonard replied.

Solanus laughed quietly and then talked to the man for quite a while, though others were also waiting outside to talk with him. Luke Leonard left the friary encouraged. He never again had an alcoholic drink, he said years later. He believed that the spiritual support of Fr. Solanus had helped to cure his "illness." Perhaps Solanus understood more about alcoholism than Luke Leonard realized. Most doctors and health authorities now believe that alcoholism is actually a disease — an "illness," as Solanus put it.

Inside the house, the Capuchins became almost accustomed to excited reports of blindness healed, deafness cured, atheism reversed. The friars themselves, however, were only rarely the recipients of the "favors" that continued to be linked with their aging porter, Solanus.

Fr. Solanus believed that he and his brother Capuchins — and all others in religious life — were not to seek healings. If they were following closely in the footsteps of Christ, sufferings were to be seen as blessings. But there were a few Capuchins apparently relieved of some burdens through the prayers of Fr. Solanus. One was Br. Daniel Brady. He developed a serious infection in the jaw while in the novitiate in 1941. The situation was worrisome, he told Fr. Solanus, but not just because he was to have surgery.

Br. Daniel was anxious because major surgery would probably force his withdrawal from the novitiate and possibly put a halt to his religious vocation. Fr. Solanus understood. He instructed the young man to kneel and blessed him right then and there. "As he did so, he touched my cheek and when he did, I knew it was healed," Br. Daniel wrote of the event in 1983. "I could feel it tighten up."

When the brother returned to his dentist, there was no sign of the dangerous infection. Feeling as though he'd received a new lease on life, Br. Daniel breezed through the front door on his trip back from the dentist. Bubbling with his good fortune, he shared the news with Solanus at his desk.

"That calls for a celebration," Fr. Solanus agreed. Then, according to Daniel, the porter grinned, yanked open a desk drawer, and produced two intact ice-cream cones — one for himself and one for Br. Daniel. A visitor had come in with them a full thirty minutes earlier. In some inexplicable way, the cones had been "preserved" from their otherwise predictable and sloppy fate!

Fr. Solanus had always had a lively appetite for fun. But he had an unending taste for quiet and meditation, too. To those coming to see him, it seemed that Fr. Solanus often moved into a zone of deeper prayer after they told him of their problems. Solanus, they said, would lean back into his chair for a moment and gaze off into a new direction. He was quiet then and would respond only after spending some time in that realm. Often, he would then make prophetic sorts of statements or give counsel.

This was momentary meditation. Fr. Solanus had discovered that his ministry needed the nourishment of much meditation. That was why his hours of rest and sleep were increasingly diminished throughout the 1930s and 1940s. It was his choice. He felt more need to feed his spirit than to rest his body.

Ironically, only illness began to provide Fr. Solanus with the bigger blocks of time for the prayer that he hungered for. Throughout the early 1940s, there were scattered bouts of illness, as the monastery chronicle noted. "September 13, 1942: Fr. Solanus was sick in bed last night; he was unable to go to his help-out at St. Paul's. Fr. Solanus was taken to St. Mary's Hospital with a 104.5 degrees temperature." The problem this time was a chronic case of eczema, a skin disease marked by itching, inflamed, and scaly skin. The legs of Fr. Solanus were severely inflamed by the eczema and were often almost raw.

On the night of September 12, trying a suggested remedy, he used the heat of an electric light near his feet, but he forgot to apply salve after turning off the light. By the morning of September 13, his legs and feet were unbearably painful and were beet-red. His fever went to 104.5 degrees and he was hospitalized at St. Mary's Hospital for about ten days. With that kind of fever and with the potential for infection, the situation was life-threatening.

It wasn't long before the people of Detroit heard that Fr. Solanus Casey was hospitalized. A rumor that he had died added to the deluge of calls and visitors the hospital had to handle. For Solanus, however, the illness was a time for penance and prayer, although a very painful time. It was a number of weeks before he could resume his full schedule at the porter's desk.

"To me it seemed about ten days of the really best penance that the poor sinner Solanus had ever gone through," Solanus wrote to his brother Jim. "The old foot is still stiff but by keeping it raised and rested, it causes very little pain," he wrote in another letter to his sister Margaret LeDoux.

By late 1942 and early 1943, there was no way for Fr. Solanus to reassure his brother Msgr. Edward about his health. Edward had returned to the Philippines. Though his family could only guess at his fate, Msgr. Casey was imprisoned by the Japanese when the islands were overrun during World War II. Solanus and the rest of the Caseys continued to pray for Ed, not knowing whether he was dead or alive. Though he missed Edward's input, Fr. Solanus continued to monitor the welfare of Fr. Maurice in Baltimore through letters and phone calls. While this was going on, Solanus learned that his seventy-eight-year-old brother Jim, who had

A message on a 1943 photo given to Edward and Selina Wollenweber of Detroit by Fr. Solanus reads: "Only in Heaven can we be satisfied as being fully and really converted. Therefore, — including the above, poor Fr. Solanus — pray for the conversion of sinners — and that God send laborers into His harvest. Fr. Solanus, O.F.M. Cap."

been in poor health for some years, had died in Seattle on January 12, 1944.

On November 25, 1944, Fr. Solanus glanced at the calendar and realized that it was his seventy-fourth birthday. Silently, he thanked God for the blessings of all those years, but his day at the monastery brought no further thought of the anniversary.

New Year's Day 1945 dawned just a few weeks later and the future looked brighter than it had for many years. The end of the war appeared imminent. In Europe and in Asia, American soldiers were achieving victories along with the other Allied forces, while Germany, Italy, and Japan were weakening.

CHAPTER NINE

Brooklyn and the Archangel's Wings
(1945–1946)

IN THE SPRING AND EARLY SUMMER of 1945, Americans were filled with great hope and a newborn confidence in the future. The war was over!

The mood among members of the large Casey clan was similarly upbeat. There was good news about sixty-five-year-old Msgr. Edward in March. He had survived four years of imprisonment in a Japanese concentration camp in the Philippines. On March 23, the Americans stormed the camp before the Japanese had time to massacre their 2,000 prisoners. Among the prisoners were 125 nuns, two bishops, and 150 priests, including Msgr. Casey. As the Casey family discovered later, their Msgr. Ed had acted courageously to protect weakened men just one day before American GIs rescued them. A Japanese officer had ordered calorie allotments to be cut from 900 to 600 calories per day. It was a killing order. Even a 900-calorie daily regime was a terrible deprivation from the 3,000-calorie daily requirement said to be optimal for men.

With immense pride in their brother, Edward, the west-coast Caseys decided to double their celebration plans for late

June in 1945. John McCluskey, son of Patrick and Genevieve McCluskey of Seattle, was to be ordained. Genevieve was the youngest of the Casey sisters and brothers, nine of whom were still living.

The west coast Caseys quickly decided that the occasion should be the largest, most joyous gathering of the Casey clan since the golden wedding anniversary of their parents in 1913. Their brother Edward had survived four years in a prisoner of war camp. There was to be a new priest in the family. There were reasons for Casey joy!

When Edward was back in the states, Owen and Patrick flew in from Seattle to welcome him. Together, the three brothers then traveled from Chicago to Detroit to see "Barney" at St. Bonaventure. At the monastery, they quickly urged him to accompany them on their trip west for the ordination of young John.

Solanus asked whether their brother, Fr. Maurice, was to accompany them as well. When Ed, Owen, and Pat said, "No," Solanus replied that he would not go if Maurice did not or could not go, pointing out that the oldest surviving Casey would be the only one not at the ordination.

Solanus's resistance surprised the three younger brothers, but they knew there was no talking him into going without Maurice. So Msgr. Edward, Owen, and Patrick Casey quickly boarded a plane bound for Baltimore. At Mt. Hope Sanitarium, they were finally able to arrange for the discharge of Fr. Maurice. (Fr. Solanus and other family members had not been favorably impressed with the course of therapy for Fr. Maurice there, anyway.) A quick message to Fr. Solanus in Detroit was all the reassurance he needed. He had already secured permission from his superiors for a vacation. In general, every friar was entitled to two weeks of vacation each year. Capuchin superiors at St. Bonaventure knew very well that, at seventy-four, Fr. Solanus could use a break from his grueling schedule.

On June 15, reported the St. Bonaventure Chronicle, Fr. Solanus left for Chicago. There, he met with his four brothers. Together, Ed, Owen, Pat, Solanus, and Maurice boarded a train for the West. At the other end of the country, the Caseys, the LeDouxes, the Bradys, and the McCluskeys waited in Seattle to gather the clan together once again.

None of the family had anticipated what the presence of Fr. Solanus would mean, however. Soon after Seattle people heard of his arrival, the phones began to ring and the living rooms began to fill with "visitors." Local pastors wanted him to say Mass in their parishes. Fr. Solanus was a "celebrity" in a city where he had never even lived.

The story was the same in other places he visited. After young John's ordination at the end of June, Solanus went on to Spokane to visit other relatives there. Then, relatives in California asked him to stay with them before returning to Detroit. Thinking that he could get a train back to Detroit from Oakland or San Francisco easily enough, Fr. Solanus agreed.

Once he was in California, however, he found that travel would be a problem. Thousands of servicemen were coming into port in San Francisco on their way home. Fr. Solanus wrote to Fr. Marion Roessler, the guardian at St. Bonaventure, that he would not be able to return by the date indicated on his "obedience." The Capuchin superior in Los Angeles tried to help but to no avail. "So here I am still — hoping to make the best of missing the privileges of the Chapter," Fr. Solanus told Fr. Marion. Solanus also expressed a hope that the order of "discipline" would not suffer at the chapter.

The "chapter" referred to a canonical meeting of superiors and delegates that met every three years to determine assignments, elect new superiors, and conduct other business of the order. This particular chapter was to make a very critical change with regard to its busiest porter, Solanus. When Fr. Solanus was finally back in Detroit, it was already Saturday, July 21. He had been gone thirty-six days, or fifteen days longer than planned. The chapter had been concluded and a new superior at St. Bonaventure's, Fr. Bernard Burke, called him in and informed him that he was being transferred quickly. His new assignment was to be at St. Michael's Friary in Brooklyn.

For twenty-one years, Solanus had been at St. Bonaventure's. He'd made hundreds of friends in Detroit; he'd grown used to, but had not been defeated by, the infirmities of old age in the Motor City. Fr. Burke noticed that Fr. Solanus received the news of this rupture most graciously. When he left Father Guardian (as the Capuchins referred to their superior), Solanus headed for his small room to pack a few things, as he had very little time to make travel connections to New York. Capuchin regulations required that the friars be in place to begin new assignments within ten days of assignment announcements at the chapter. But the chapter changes had been posted at 10:00 A.M. on July 15 — while Fr. Solanus was still in California. Nevertheless, he was bound by obedience to be at St. Michael's by 10:00 A.M. on July 25, which gave him only two or three days to move.

This was certainly not the first time that Solanus had been told to pull up his roots and relocate. It was, as he knew very well, part of religious life. It was also definitely part of the Franciscan spirit — no personal attachments, even to a city of people he'd loved so deeply through the years of the Great

Depression and World War II. Nonetheless, people in Detroit who heard about his move wondered if such a transfer wasn't a bit hard on a man now in his seventy-fifth year. The truth was, his age was only one of the concerns that the Capuchin superiors had in mind in making the change.

As a sort of prayer for his family, but especially for Maurice, Fr. Solanus had begun to reread *The Mystical City of God* by Mary of Agreda. He'd become increasingly attached to this devotional work since first reading it in 1924 and recommended to many people over the years. Some people became almost as devoted to the Agreda volumes as he was. But in the eyes of some within the Church, Mary of Agreda's book was merely an apocryphal work, not at all worthy of endorsement by priests or other Church authorities. The extreme length of the work (about 600 pages for the first three volumes, nearly 800 for the fourth), and its questionable value in the eyes of some priests, were controversies in themselves. But soon, officials at the Detroit chancery office began hearing complaints from some that a Capuchin was "promoting" a book which was not only expensive but a burden to read.

Finally, in 1943–1944, the Capuchin superiors came to a point where they had to insist that Fr. Solanus separate himself from a group of supporters who had become extremely attached to him and to *The Mystical City of God*. A man named Ray Garland was at the center of some *Mystical City* devotees. He was also totally devoted to Fr. Solanus, whom he had met in 1927. Later, when Fr. Solanus began to help out with weekend liturgies at St. Paul's Maltese Parish in Detroit, Garland and company followed. They attended the Masses Fr. Solanus had and set up breakfast meetings after the Mass to study the Agreda volumes. But there was an intensity about the piety of this group that others saw as unhealthy. When Solanus was in the hospital and unable to attend their Sunday meetings, they continued to meet at St. Paul's themselves, despite the wishes of the pastor that they meet only when Fr. Solanus himself was present for meetings.

Finally, Fr. Solanus was ordered to tell Ray Garland not to come to St. Bonaventure's to visit anymore. Though Fr. Solanus told his superiors that he felt Garland was being misunderstood, he was thoroughly obedient. But Garland apparently continued to telephone, short-circuiting the Capuchin superiors in a way Solanus found hard to rebuff. Garland was calling to seek the spiritual counsel of Solanus for himself and for the Agreda circle, but Capuchins did not wish to foster any sort of "personality cult" and believed that Solanus was being manipulated. It was time to protect both the man and the man's health.

That's how Solanus found himself on his way east to Brooklyn. He was to be porter — although in semiretirement — there at St. Michael's Friary.

Before his Detroit friends knew that Fr. Solanus was back from California, he was already beginning to make himself at home at 225 Jerome Street in Brooklyn. When he looked around, he quickly noticed the massive statue of St. Michael, a landmark near the church and friary. He described it to others as a very protective monument.

Though the news of his departure may have been devastating for many in Detroit, to many friars at St. Bonaventure's, the transfer of Fr. Solanus was just another transfer.

"It was kind of a surprise for the community and the people," recalled Fr. Cosmas Niedhammer, then novice master for the brothers' novitiate. "However, I was hardly conscious of it.

I know he was simply told to go, and went. I know the rest of the community hardly noticed either."

Fr. Solanus, meanwhile, looked forward to becoming reacquainted with the concept of "relaxing." In a note back to St. Bonaventure's, written soon after he was established at St. Michael's, he confided that he'd been worn out and was relieved to move.

Solanus also wrote to St. Bonaventure's Br. Leo Wollenweber — a brother in his early twenties who'd been named to help with portering duties in the early 1940s — and asked him to send along a few personal belongings he'd had no time to pack. Among the things he wanted sent was a copy of a small prayer he hoped to have duplicated for distribution to those wanting it.

"I hope to get a little more time for such things here at St. Michael's," Fr. Solanus told Br. Leo on July 30. "I've taken a little more sleep under the great archangel's wings this past week than perhaps in three weeks before my arrival." The weeks Solanus was thinking of were those busy weeks he'd spent visiting, meeting, and counseling people out west while he was "on vacation"! Within eight days, he had spanned the width of the country, traveling up and down the West Coast and then on to St. Paul, Detroit, and finally to New York.

But if many of his Capuchin brothers hardly noticed the departure of Fr. Solanus, St. Michael's knew that something was very different within a month.

Before long, friends from Detroit learned of his whereabouts. Some began to write to him, others planned to travel the 600 miles to Brooklyn just to talk with him. A Mrs. Edward Wolfe, of Brighton, Michigan, couldn't wait to do either. She called.

Doctors had told Mrs. Wolfe that her baby daughter, Kathleen, was suffering from celiac disease, an ailment in which food is incompletely absorbed in the intestines, thus contributing to malnutrition. Little Kathleen was literally starving to death despite her mother's best efforts to feed her. The doctors had nothing more to offer the child.

When Fr. Solanus had heard enough of the story from Mrs. Wolfe over the phone, he asked her to kneel down, holding the baby in one arm, and then blessed the baby "over the phone." He also asked her mother to spend the money she would have spent in coming to Brooklyn to do something for those in need. Soon, Baby Kathleen's disease started to regress. She began to digest food normally and was on the road to recovery.

With little in the way of official responsibilities, Solanus did some sightseeing and visiting in the autumn of 1945. New York parishes, after all, had been his first assignments as a priest, and he'd grown to love the city people. He thoroughly enjoyed returning to Sacred Heart for the annual Labor Day picnic; he still loved the hot dogs with onions, the beer, the games that were part of the parish festival fun. There were even still a few who'd heard of the seventy-four-year-old from his years of ministry there before World War I.

But back at St. Michael's, the hours of leisure disappeared as summer cooled and autumn overtook it. If there were fewer people to meet and talk with at St. Michael's door, there were many more to counsel by mail and over the phone. Every night, Solanus took pen in hand and wrote to as many people as his tired eyes and head could permit. Often, he did not quit until after midnight.

Little stacks of three-by-five postcards, his customary stationery, would be filled up with his responses often written in green ink — a Casey family preference. They were mailed out the next day, but that did not mean that Fr. Solanus had reached the bottom of his pile of "letters to be answered." That reality was very frustrating to him.

"I must be about fifty letters behind — quite some not opened," he wrote to his sister Margaret in Oakland. "Pray the Lord give some system or other whereby I keep up."

Among those letters Fr. Solanus had to answer was a pack from Ray Garland and the Agreda group in Detroit.

"I must tell you something that, in a way, I do not like to do," Fr. Solanus wrote to him, trying to broach a painful subject in a considerate fashion. "It is this. The arch-enemy of our Blessed Mother and of immortal souls — at all times on the alert — must have received an extra length of rope these days. I have been reported as having been phoning long distance to you and the 'Agredan Society.'"

The situation was giving "offense, if not scandal" to his Capuchin superiors, Fr. Solanus explained to Ray Garland. Because of that, he asked Garland to "leave me out of the picture" until all the misunderstandings were cleared up. It was, most probably, a painful message for Fr. Solanus to write. He was never convinced that the Garland group was at all misled in their interest in *The Mystical City of God*. But he was obedient to the orders of his superiors and always ready to listen to their advice. The Garland connection was severed.

If Fr. Solanus was bothered by the forced end of this friendship, he did not show it. In fact, he worked hard at establishing a rapport with the Capuchins at St. Michael's. To some degree, his reputation as a priest of great virtue and great spiritual ministry had preceded him. But that was not enough to endear him as a musician during recreation time, as several of his fellow priests recalled:

> Solanus decided to entertain the friars at their regular Sunday recreation time. So he came in with his violin. The friars thought, "Well, he is an old man trying to entertain us." So they put up with his squeaking on the violin. Their reaction seemed so positive to Solanus that he thought he had done very well. The next Sunday night, he showed up with his violin again. As he began to play, one of them went to the radio and kept turning up the volume. Without saying a word, Solanus left the room and went down before the Blessed Sacrament and continued his playing there.

Perhaps Fr. Solanus should not have been surprised. His "virtuosity" with the violin had never earned him much respect. Even Casey family members complained when he'd taken up the fiddle as a youngster. Apparently, he never got any better at it, except possibly in the all-accepting eyes of heaven, but fiddling hymns in the chapel provided a respite from the increasing burden of correspondence and visitors which Fr. Solanus found facing him in the autumn and winter months of 1945.

He did find enough time during the winter to write some of his friends and send them a small Christmas verse he had composed years earlier. It was entitled "Always Christmas Eve." The short verse suggested that the heart of each man and woman could become a "crib" which receives the infant:

> With love and Christmas greetings to all
> Comes the Infant once more to free us from sorrow

Whose smile and whose power and whose gentleness
    call
To each heart and each soul for a manger tomorrow;
Whose love and whose goodness
— whose wonders proclaim
Him, the Son of the Virgin, as promised of yore.
Oh, may he estrange us from sin and its shame!
And reign in our hearts, as his crib evermore!

Now he added this reflection:

. . . Ah, the rest of us, on Calvary
Mary conceived under the Cross
Thirty-three years later. Glory to God!
Peace to men of GOOD WILL.

With World War II finally ended, Christmas 1945 was a joyous one. In New York, Solanus sent out his Christmas verse with greetings and also tried to keep up with the increasing requests for his blessings and counsel. More and more, as the snow fell on Brooklyn, bundled-up visitors rang the doorbell at St. Michael's. And yet, he found the crush of visitors and the strain considerably less than it had been in Detroit.

"I do have perhaps hours as long but it's a change," Solanus wrote to his brother Edward. "Here it's correspondence that takes most of the time. There, I simply had to leave most of that to others. And while I meet with pathetic cases to solve or try to alleviate, the strain and tension is by no means so pressing."

Over the years, Solanus had found a few ways to "escape" from the crush when the circumstances allowed for it. Serving as part-time porter at St. Michael's provided more of these opportunities to "escape." He would often sneak a nap beneath the large porter's desk when "business" was slow. Since he often did not go to bed until midnight and rose at 4:30 A.M. or so, the naps were not an old man's self-indulgence. If the phone rang or the doorbell buzzed, Solanus bounced up, dusted his habit off, smoothed his hair back into place, and resumed the dignified demeanor of a porter always at his post.

One of those who rang the bell at St. Michael's one day was the mother of Barnabas Keck, a Capuchin seminarian. He had met Solanus at the seminary in Garrison, New York. Mrs. Ruth Keck had already consulted someone about her problem. Her doctor had implied, but refused to tell her, that she was suffering from cancer. Her son later told the story of her meeting with Fr. Solanus.

"When my mother's turn came, Fr. Solanus said, 'And what's your problem, dear?'

"'I think I have cancer,' she said.

"All he said was, 'Don't you know God can cure cancer just like a toothache?' So she knelt down and he put his hand on her and blessed her, praying over her."

She went home and never went back to the doctor — and was eighty years old when the story was repeated in 1983.

Such news traveled fast, especially in a large metropolitan area like New York. The lines of people waiting to talk with the porter at St. Michael's began to get longer and longer as the new year of 1946 began. Within six months of his arrival at St. Michael's, Capuchin superiors were already considering another transfer for Fr. Solanus Casey. They had suspected that St. Michael's wings might be only temporary shelter for him, and that he would simply not have a chance to rest there.

On April 26, 1946, the chronicle, or log, of St. Michael's in New York noted that Solanus was being transferred to St. Felix Friary in rural Huntington, Indiana. The Capuchins had moved their novitiate to St. Felix, which they had built in 1929. It was a friary surrounded by farmlands; even within their own grounds, the friars maintained their own orchard, vineyards, beehives, and a large vegetable garden. Fr. Maurice Joachim had begun his own Capuchin novitiate there, and Fr. Solanus had accompanied him there. After that, Solanus had been there on retreat or to get away from the Detroit routine.

So, although transfers were almost always announced after the chapters, which took place every three years, Solanus's superiors decided to place him immediately in a friary that would be farther from their larger metropolitan locations — friaries in Detroit, New York, Milwaukee. In Huntington, life might slow down for Fr. Solanus.

His superiors therefore assigned him to complete retirement; after forty years, his job as a porter had come to an end.

CHAPTER TEN

"Retirement" in Huntington
(1946–1956)

THOUGH HE SAID NOTHING about it, in his heart of hearts Fr. Solanus Casey may well have been relieved by this transfer. Life at St. Felix would be close to farmlands and fields — and to God. The handsome, sprawling brick novitiate with Spanish-tiled roof was surrounded by thirty acres of friary land, and Solanus could find a sermon in every square yard of ground.

Solanus had been born in a setting of wide-open spaces seventy-five years earlier. Most of his life, however, had been lived in large metropolitan areas. His superiors no doubt determined that it would be good to give the man a chance to enjoy the open air, now that he was to be retired. On the other hand, they also knew that Fr. Solanus was a man content with whatever came; he was good at being a religious.

In keeping with the spirit of St. Francis, which saw each friar in the same fair light, the chronicle at St. Felix in Huntington made note of his coming in a very matter-of-fact manner. "April 25. Fr. Solanus arrived from St. Michael's, Brooklyn, with an obedience to be stationed here."

By the time Fr. Solanus had settled in at St. Felix in the last days of April, spring was very much in the air. The Capuchin orchards were beginning to bud, promising a bountiful crop of apples, pears, peaches, and plums. But as the friary chronicle later noted, near the middle of May, Old Man Winter returned and threatened to ruin the crops. The friars, including the newcomer Solanus, were concerned. The recording friar's notes read:

> May 13. Fr. Dominic's mother died this evening. Last Saturday when the daily papers announced the approach of frosts, the friars thought of lighting a smudge to save the tiny apples. Fr. Solanus volunteered to bless the orchard instead with the oration 'Ad Omnia' and one to Bl. Ignatius, Capuchin Brother. Now it appears that only the grapes froze. When all around us the neighboring apples were destroyed — ours were unharmed.

Fr. Solanus had called upon the special protection of Blessed Ignatius of Laconi because that Saturday, May 11, was the feast of the good Capuchin brother. Five years after helping to "frost-proof" the apples at St. Felix, Ignatius was canonized.

If Solanus took some time to walk the grounds, most of his time was still occupied with correspondence. By May, much of what had been sent to St. Michael's in recent months was catching up with him.

"God bless you and yours," Fr. Solanus wrote, beginning a May 22 letter to a correspondent from Oswego, New York. "I hope this finds you well and that the 'kind of mixup' caused by my transfer hither, etc., may not be so grave as to be insurmountable."

Solanus was aware that many in New York might have been disappointed that they could no longer visit him in Brooklyn — just as Detroiters had been distressed about his transfer to New York. Gradually, he saw that a few people came not for his counsel on growing closer to the Lord, but for what he could do *for* them. But Solanus did not make a secret of the location of his new residence. His correspondence went out on friary notepaper, carrying the address "St. Felix Friary, Route 8, Huntington, Indiana."

In general, however, the other friars at St. Felix understood that it was best to say little about the presence of Fr. Solanus Casey to those outside their house, as he was there for retirement. And yet, Solanus could admit that his "Retirement" was still a bit taxing.

Fr. Solanus with visitors, Huntington, c. 1954.

Since my transfer from St. Bonaventure's my personal callers have been by no means as heavy; though my letters — possibly because I have to take care of them myself — seem as heavy as ever; and you can imagine how I appreciate it to have someone like one of the Brothers or Fathers in Detroit continue their generous assistence [sic] in the work that, even with such help, often keeps me — with other duties — from 5 o'cl [sic] a.m. to 11 p.m.

In late June, Solanus received word that his younger brother Augustine (Gus) had died in Seattle at the age of seventy. He drew some consolation from learning that, two days before Gus died, he had been reconciled with his brother, Patrick. For some time, there had been bitter feelings between the two. Fr. Solanus had urged both of his brothers to forgive and forget, and the healing had apparently taken place.

But Solanus was grieved over the loss of Gus, wishing that he had been able to have more contact with him. One of the burdens of his ministry had been the trouble he had in finding time to keep in touch with the large and active Casey clan. Fortunately, his new location in Indiana was more accessible for Maurice and Edward than Brooklyn had been. By now, Edward was based in Minnesota, working for the Philippine missions. Fr. Maurice was also in Minnesota, cheerfully serving in semiretirement as chaplain at a Catholic hospital in Graceville.

In September, as the house chronicle indicates, Msgr. Edward and Fr. Maurice came down to visit Fr. Solanus at St. Felix. They stayed over and walked with him through the orchards that Solanus had already glowingly described to his sister Margaret as "bountifully loaded."

The seasons passed quietly in Huntington, and the friars celebrated Advent and Christmas with great joy. In January, however, there was another reason to celebrate.

On Saturday, January 25, 1947, the *Detroit News*, a Detroit daily, printed a short article about Fr. Solanus. It announced that he was visiting the city from his new residence in Huntington, Indiana, in order to celebrate his fifty years as a Capuchin. He had entered the order on January 14, 1897. The *News* also stated that the major celebration of this anniversary would be held at St. Bonaventure's on the following day, Sunday, January 26.

Until this printed announcement of his return to Detroit, few of his Detroit admirers even knew where he was living. Fewer still knew that his golden jubilee celebration was close at hand. But that small announcement in the paper had an effect just as large if it had appeared in large type on the front page with a picture of Solanus!

St. Bonaventure's chapel was packed during the golden jubilee liturgy. Solanus noted the crowd with gratitude but could not help wandering back in memory to that cold January fourteenth in 1897. He'd walked into this same church. It was colder then, lacking the amenities of a more efficient heating system. He'd been kneeling, consumed with anxiety and doubts. He'd had knots in his stomach as he stood up to take off his suitcoat. Then the heavy brown hooded habit of these Capuchins had been placed over his head — which, at that time, was still covered with plenty of dark hair — and he received his new name, "Fr. Francis Solanus Casey." With the habit, he was given peace.

Solanus watched then as his brother, Msgr. Edward, mounted the pulpit to preach about his fifty years of service.

Part of the Casey clan gathered for Fr. Solanus's Golden Jubilee as a Capuchin priest: From left, Owen Casey of Seattle; Msgr. Edward Casey of St. Paul, Minnesota; Fr. Solanus; and Mrs. Bernard (Grace Casey) Brady, also of Seattle.

Edward had told him that the homily would be based on the Scripture verse "To those who love God, all things work together for good." Solanus leaned back to listen.

After the liturgy, those attending were handed a small card as a memento of the occasion. On the back was a message from Fr. Solanus. He had written, polished, and changed it a dozen times while a nervous friar had stood nearby, anxious to get the text over to the print shop. The message read:

PAX ET BONUM
IN MEMORY OF MY
GOLDEN JUBILEE IN RELIGION

St. Bonaventure's Monastery
Detroit, Michigan
Thanks be to God for uncountable
mercies — for every blessing!
Thanks be to my neighbor for his charitable patience.

Fifty years in the Order — almost unnoticed — have slipped
away from me into eternity. Thither I hope to follow before
half another fifty: trusting in the merciful goodness of God!

Fr. Solanus, O.F.M. Cap.
DEO GRATIAS

A dinner was held after the Mass to celebrate the event at the Third Order Hall, just down the block from St. Bonaventure's. After the dinner, Fr. Solanus, Msgr. Edward, Fr. Maurice, their brother Owen, and their sister, Mrs. Grace Brady, went to a large room above the hall for a reception. More than 2,000 people filed through a reception line, greeting, hugging, and giving money and gifts of all kinds to Fr. Solanus. The crowd that had assembled with so little publicity was awesome. Capuchin authorities, standing just out of the limelight occupied by Fr. Solanus, took note of the numbers and agreed: Fr. Solanus was better off in Huntington, a little farther from the hundreds of people who knew him but who also tired him.

Even in the reception line, many people were trying to update the guest of honor on the progress or difficulties in their lives. As always, Solanus listened keenly and did the best he could to respond. It took several hours before everyone crowding into the reception line had a chance to say a word or two to Fr. Solanus.

Two or three days later, Solanus, Ed, and Maurice saw their siblings Owen and Grace off to Seattle. Then, on February 1, after his other guests had left, Fr. Solanus returned to Huntington, driven by his good friends from Chicago, Joseph and Winifred O'Donnell. The O'Donnell car also carried the many gifts given to Solanus. These included vestments, an alb, altar linens, money, and a chalice. Though Solanus appreciated the love and affection he received, he hardly knew what to do with the many gifts that people increasingly showered upon him. After asking permission, he later gave the chalice to a visiting missionary bishop serving in India.

Notice of his Huntington residence in the Detroit paper increased the numbers of visitors headed there. It also quickly doubled and tripled the mail coming into St. Felix Friary, most of which was addressed to "Fr. Solanus Casey." Facing daily mini-mountains of mail, Fr. Solanus had taken up typing somewhere along the line. But his typing speed was poor and served primarily to spare his hands. With age, his hands became more arthritic, making it hard for him to hold a pen.

His Huntington days typically started at 4:15 or 4:30 A.M., though the community was not awakened until the 4:55 sounding of the wooden clappers. The friar assigned to the task of awakening the others slapped the wooden blocks together, announcing "*Surgite, Fratres*" ("Arise, brothers"). It was the same daily awakening routine that Solanus had heard since his entry into the order as Barney Casey Jr. a half-century earlier.

After rising, Solanus would slip his habit over his head, pull on his sandals, and head for the chapel. He liked to pray alone there until the rest of the community gathered at 5:15 for morning prayers. A community Mass followed at 6:15. Afterward was breakfast, eaten in silence. The odd practice Solanus still had of mixing his coffee, orange juice, and cereal into one strange-looking breakfast stew must have made the silence a challenge for the novices.

At 8:00 A.M., Solanus slipped into the chapel again to attend the Mass celebrated for the novices in residence and in schooling at St. Felix. After Mass, he lingered in prayer in the chapel until 9:15 or 9:30, the time the postman usually came with the sacks of mail from the Huntington Post Office.

By 9:30 in the morning, Solanus had already been up for more than five hours. His workday started then, as mail was opened and sorted. Much of the mail related to requests for enrollment in the Seraphic Mass Association, for which Solanus was the friary director. There was money in many of the letters Solanus had to open. Not long after he returned from Detroit and his golden jubilee, Fr. Matthias, the Capuchin guardian, appointed Fr. Herbert to help Solanus with correspondence.

Fr. Ambrose De Groot, then about thirty-nine, was assigned to St. Felix in the summer of 1946. From what he heard, Fr. Solanus needed help badly.

"Naturally, it was just too much for him to take care of all this correspondence. Money for Seraphic Mass enrollments and stipend money for Masses would frequently be found buried in the pile of mail on his desk. It wasn't that he was careless. He just wasn't a legalist so that he found reason to worry about these matters. . . . It even took Fr. Solanus forever just to write his name on an SMA card. Fr. Herbert also made replies to all these requests. But if the person sought any personal advice from Fr. Solanus, this, of course was left to him."

Letters could be stacked up to be answered later; phone calls and visitors at the friary door couldn't.

"The phone rang continually — and almost every time, the party at the other end of the line asked to speak with Fr. Solanus," Fr. De Groot recalled. "Sometimes we would have to search all over the grounds for him. Perhaps he would be out walking — or running around the orchard, which he loved to do for exercise. Old as he was, he was wiry and limber. The doorbell too was ringing constantly for him. Cars came from almost every state in the union and from Canada. He took his time with each person who came to him. He listened to their problems. And undoubtedly he helped them. He must have done *something* for them. Or else his clientele would have faded out. But it didn't."

When called away from what he was doing, Fr. Solanus, as the younger Fr. De Groot observed him, "never showed impatience or resentment. And . . . [his patience] must have been tried many times." Perhaps in response to the overload, Fr. Solanus escaped to "outdoor ministries." In the garden or on the lawn, he could be silent. It was very satisfying to tend to growing things — or to the beehives, in which he took a special interest, as shown in this entry in the St. Felix chronicle for May 8, 1947:

> Some bees arrived today from Dadant Co. in Illinois. Fr. Master and Solanus put them in their new home. Several weeks ago the old bees had been discontented with our hospitality and decided to pull up stakes for a better place. So they swarmed and left us empty-handed. When the new bees arrived, it was found that the queen was dead. Fr. Solanus immediately called the company and asked for another.

Though he was going on seventy-seven, Fr. Solanus remained in relatively stable health during the summer of 1947. Around Huntington, he was occasionally seen visiting the Victory Noll Sisters, as Our Lady of Victory Missionary Sisters are popularly called. Founded by Fr. John Sigsteen — and subsequently supported by Archbishop John F. Noll, the bishop of the diocese and founder of the Catholic publishing house Our Sunday Visitor, Inc. — the Victory Noll Sisters had their motherhouse just two miles from the monastery.

Often Fr. Solanus would go with some of the other Capuchins to Victory Noll when they went to hear the confessions for the sisters. Solanus would simply sit and talk to the nuns, enjoying their company.

In June, Bernard Casey, a nephew of Fr. Solanus, came to visit for a few days from San Francisco. He'd been in the service during the war and wanted to get to know his uncle a little before settling in to civilian life.

In the autumn, Solanus was still active inside and outside the friary. While visitors and loads of letters preoccupied much of his day in his small office at St. Felix, he continued to hoe in the garden, attack weeds in the lawn, and serve as assistant beekeeper. In late December, however, the skin problem with his legs flared up again. This time, the house chronicle noted on December 31, the flare-up was vicious.

> We gave our annual spiritual bouquet to Father Guardian this evening after supper. Fr. Damasus gave the talk . . . and he surprised us all. It was very nice. Recreation this evening. Fr. Solanus has been ill for several days already. He has a skin disease on his legs. He could not say Mass this morn-

ing, and there seems little chance for immediate improvement. Seems to be getting worse.

The chronicler was making no overstatement. The ailments Fr. Solanus suffered from were becoming worse. His
superiors could assume that his pain and discomfort had
become acute when he admitted that he could not rise to say
Mass. If there was any way to put up with his inflamed legs,
Solanus would say Mass.

By January 25, 1948, the chronicle added, "Fr. Solanus
came to dinner today in the refectory — the first time in many
days. He is feeling better but is still far from well." Even on the
days before he was down for dinner, however, Solanus was
doing what he could to get letters out. One went to his niece ,
Mrs. Aurelia Herkenrath, who was experiencing problems with
her hearing. Her uncle told her that he had enrolled her in the
Seraphic Mass Association. His concluding words contained a
familiar message:

> I think it would help if you made a proposition to the Poor
> Souls — including your relatives specially — that you will
> enroll them most specilly [sic], say for a small % of the Dr. bill
> if your hearing improves without treatment so as to surprise
> the doctors. Then have as many as possible to offer holy com-
> munion often. Fr. Sol.

By Holy Week, 1948, Fr. Solanus had rebounded again. On
Good Friday, he served as subdeacon at services and as deacon at
the Easter liturgy on Sunday, March 28. Within another ten days,
he was able to watch Br. Harold plowing the fields outside. His
fellow friars at St. Felix now had recognized a quick way to assess

the condition of his legs. "If he ran up the stairs," one friar noted, "we knew he was feeling well, but if he seemed to lumber along, then we knew that his legs were giving him a lot of trouble."

On June 6, Fr. Herbert, who had been helping Fr. Solanus, was getting ready to leave for Montana, but the Capuchins were not about to leave Solanus without an assistant. On June 9, Fr. Blase Gitzen arrived from Detroit. Newly ordained, Fr. Blase had served as an altar boy for Solanus many years earlier. He remembered Solanus as the very pious priest who always took so much longer to say Mass.

Fr. Blase was assigned to serve as full-time secretary for Fr. Solanus. With his young eyes and energy, it was hoped that much of the burden of the correspondence could be lifted from the aging, weakening shoulders of Solanus. Young Fr. Blase prepared to roll up his sleeves and roll paper into the office typewriter. However, he noticed right off that there were a few things askew which he wanted to straighten out.

"In some ways he offended my Prussian regularity and orderliness," Fr. Blase said of Fr. Solanus, in an interview given many years later. "He had money on him (which he just stuffed into his habit pockets) and money all over the room (which he stuffed into the cubby holes of his desk, or used as page markers). And he didn't know to which account that money was to be credited.

"So one day, with the blessing of the superior, I went through his room and collected $153. He never said anything, but I got the impression that he wasn't very pleased that I cleaned up his room. Not that he cared about the money. He never took care of it because he just couldn't care less. But I lost his place in many a book!"

During the summer of 1948, Fr. Blase also began to set up more of a routine for handling the incoming mail. He would open the thirty to forty letters which Solanus received each day. Blase would then record money received and sort the letters. In one stack were letters he thought might require only a simple acknowledgment. In the other stack, however, were the heart-wrenching stories of people desperate for some spiritual consolation and prayer. Blase "prayed" that Fr. Solanus would reply to these himself. And Solanus typically did. As Blase remembered:

> In the course of the day, I would receive the answers he had crashed out on an old battered typewriter. They were typed mostly on three-by-five cards. The spelling was bad, pure fifth-grade stuff, but the contents simply amazed me. With a few words he was able to come to the heart of the problem. His understanding of people, his sympathetic response, his grasp of theology just astounded me.

In the late afternoon, Fr. Solanus and many of the other friars were working outdoors. Sometimes, Solanus was out after the dandelions in the lawn. But at other times, he was involved in more serious efforts. On July 27, as the chronicle reported, "Fr. Master with Fr. Solanus's help extracted 40 lbs. of honey from one of the hives." The queen bee ordered by Solanus during the previous year had managed to get things going quite successfully.

Bees fascinated Fr. Solanus. He was often noticed by some of the other friars near the apiary. One or two bees would crawl up and down his welcoming fingers as he "preached" some sort of outdoor sermon to them. Occasionally, he was stung, but his admiration for the "marvelous things" wasn't diminished.

One time, after finding a bee in his office, he coaxed the thing onto his finger and headed for the window to set it free. But Solanus found that the screen couldn't be budged. At just that moment, Frater Leon had the misfortune to pass by. Solanus called him in and transferred the bee to Leon's hand because Leon's legs were younger and quicker. Leon was a bit skeptical about escorting a bee but couldn't refuse Fr. Solanus. The young man made it down the corridor and almost to the outside friary door. Then, he got the bee's point!

In September 1948, the house guardian, Fr. Matthias, died. A week later, Fr. Herbert (the Capuchin who had helped Fr. Solanus with his mail several years earlier) was named the new guardian. He knew very well how taxing the office work and visitors were on Solanus. The one-time porter was now almost seventy-eight years old. During the autumn and winter, however, Fr. Solanus remained in good health and was very active.

On January 12, 1949, Fr. Solanus received sad news. Msgr. Edward called to tell him that Fr. Maurice Joachim had died. Maurice was eighty-one years old. Coincidentally, Jim Casey, the oldest Casey son, had died on the same date, January 12, in 1944.

As a brother, Fr. Solanus felt the loss of Maurice keenly. He had suffered with the trials experienced by Fr. Maurice for many years. Through dozens of phone calls and hundreds of hours of letter-writing and talking, Solanus had tried to help Fr. Maurice find a joy and peace in the gifts God had given him.

As a believer, however, Solanus was happy for the new life Maurice could now enjoy. Up in Graceville, Minnesota, several days later, it was Fr. Solanus who gave the homily at his older brother's funeral liturgy. He spoke of death as a humiliating but purifying gateway to eternal life. Death, he told the congregation, "is the last of the blessings God showers upon our earthly journey toward home." It was his favorite theme — gratitude to God for whatever He gives to us.

Solanus himself was best suited to know how difficult that had been for Maurice. Maurice had suffered humiliations just to become a priest. He had failed in the seminary at an early age and had then returned after he saw Barney ordained. Later, Maurice had sincerely believed that he could serve best as a Capuchin. But even that assurance faded. He finally left the order and later felt misunderstood and frustrated as a priest. Clearly burdened by mental and emotional problems, Maurice had known very little peace until the very end of his life.

Soon after the funeral, Fr. Solanus sat one day in his Huntington office and told a Detroit visitor, Miss Agnes O'Neil, about his brother's death. Death, he told her, should be seen as one of the happiest experiences of human life. Miss O'Neil, one of the many people healed of an illness through the prayers of Fr. Solanus, considered what the old Capuchin had just told her. Nevertheless, she was grateful to him for having asked God to cure her.

In February, all the men at St. Felix listened for the news about Cardinal Jozsef Mindszenty, the primate of Hungary. Cardinal Mindszenty had been charged with treason and put on trial by the Communist government in Budapest. The fifty-six-year-old pastor of the Church in Hungary was convicted and sentenced to life in prison. Solanus found the proceedings and the outcome a horrendous injustice and a commentary on the fruits of an atheistic government. In late April 1949, Fr. Solanus, along with Frs. Ambrose, Angelus, and Herbert from

St. Felix, set out for Milwaukee by car. They were headed for the unveiling of a statue of a Capuchin, Fr. Stephen Eckert, who had died there in 1923. Solanus had known him in Yonkers at Sacred Heart, in 1904. He had been so impressed with the holiness of Fr. Stephen that he worked with others to promote Fr. Stephen's cause for beatification.

On the way up to Milwaukee, Fr. Solanus suggested that they stop in Chicago to see his friends, the O'Donnells. He assured the other friars that it would be no problem for the O'Donnells to give them a bit of dinner. The other three weren't prepared for the lavish "spread" and the deference they received in a rather grand setting. Fr. Ambrose De Groot told of the incident years later:

> It turned out they were wealthy people who lived in one of the high-rise apartments along Lake Shore Drive. We found ourselves ushered into a beautifully furnished apartment overlooking Lake Michigan, many stories [up] from the ground level.
>
> I personally felt embarrassed, calling on these people unannounced, and expecting an invitation to supper. I was rather amazed to see these people brighten up when they saw Fr. Solanus. They felt sincerely honored and just could not do enough for us. They called a caterer and had a beautiful dinner sent to the apartment. It was borrowed glory as far as I and the rest of us were concerned. It was Fr. Solanus all the way — the wealthy couple just hung on his words. . . . Fr. Solanus took it all in stride and just did not notice the fuss made over him. To him these were simply good people who had told him that he would always be welcome in their home.

Another meal the four friars ate a few days later in Milwaukee was also memorable, but certainly not in the same way. Solanus almost died as a result of it.

At St. Benedict's, where the statue of Fr. Stephen was dedicated, a ham dinner was served. Solanus was allergic to ham and seldom ate any of it, but, in honor of the occasion, he decided to try a little. This ham, however, was spoiled, and a large number of people became ill with food poisoning. Having a more violent reaction to it than others, Solanus had to be rushed to St. Michael's Hospital where, for awhile, he was in serious condition.

Though the four returned to St. Felix Friary on April 29, Solanus was still not feeling well, and the friars noticed that he was walking instead of running up the stairs.

On May 6, Fr. Solanus had to be hospitalized at St. Joseph's Hospital in Fort Wayne. His doctors had diagnosed the condition as "weeping eczema," and when the disease was at its worst, the legs of the former porter were covered with painful open sores. The doctors told Fr. Solanus that they might have to amputate his legs this time. There was very little circulation in the raw, inflamed legs. When Fr. Blase, Solanus's secretary, came to see him, however, he found that the threat of amputation wasn't really preoccupying Solanus. Visitors were!

It was decided by the friars that word of his hospitalization would not be mentioned. We knew he was seriously ill, and we wanted him to get some rest. To my utter surprise, despite a big "DO NOT DISTURB" sign on the door, I found fifteen people in the room the next day when I visited him. Some had come from as far away as Detroit. How they found him, I'll never know. But here he was, propped up in bed, with a white canopy over his legs, amiably chatting with his visitors. And sure enough, every three minutes, a disapproving nurse came in to check the pulse in his legs.

His attitude toward his illness was one of such lack of concern, that I was curious whether he knew how seriously ill he had been and brought up the subject on the way home from the hospital. Yes, he knew that his legs might have to be amputated, but he had the attitude: "If they came off, it was alright; if not, that was alright too."

Solanus remained in Fort Wayne in the hospital until May 22. Warm weather, and the prospect of another season as assistant beekeeper and senior gardener, may have speeded his recovery. In one part of the garden at St. Felix, he had also been cultivating a patch of wild strawberries which he told the friars he was "taming." After eating them, the friars agreed that the "taming" was successful: the berries were delicious!

By the summer of 1949, Fr. Solanus had been stationed at Huntington for a little over three years. It was enough time for his many friends to discover just how many miles Huntington was from Detroit, from Chicago, or even from Yonkers, New York.

The Capuchin strategy of sending Solanus to an out-of-the-way location turned out to be only partially successful. People in chartered buses came down from Detroit to see him, especially during the summer months. The celebration of Corpus Christi — and the name day of Fr. Solanus (St. Francis Solano on July 21) — provided other reasons for the caravans of his friends to arrive. St. Felix would host the visitors to Mass (including a Solanus *ferverino*) and then some light refreshment. Then the busloads full of people would reboard the buses and start the five- to six-hour trip home.

Huntington, a small town of about 15,000, also sensed that there was something unusual, something special, about one of the priests at the friary. So did the Victory Noll sisters.

"At Victory Noll, we used to get so many calls and visitors, even in the middle of the night," recalled a Victory Noll nun. "People from Chicago or Detroit, from all around the country, would come to us, mistaking Victory Noll for St. Felix Friary, where Fr. Solanus lived." Eventually, she said, local cabdrivers caught on to the confusion outsiders often had. They'd cut right through the muddle over Victory Noll and St. Felix and ask their fares: "Do you want to go to the Victory Noll for men or for women?" Throughout the remainder of 1949 and into 1950, Fr. Solanus coped with his workload as best he could. He was nearing eighty and his skin condition and varicose veins made it increasingly difficult to stay as active as he wanted to be. He had always been an advocate of "keeping in trim," as he put it, and being careful about his diet.

Eating fresh vegetables and fruits was necessary to stay in good shape, Solanus often reminded the other friars and the novices at St. Felix. Many of them were city boys and not so enthused about his dietary philosophies. One "home remedy" for which he found no support at all was walking barefoot in the friary yard, even during cold weather. He believed it stimulated the circulation in his problem legs.

When he was able, he would play volleyball or tennis with the novices. And when he played, he played with total enthusiasm and no holding back. When he fell down, he would pick himself up and continue. If Solanus had any favorite indoor pastime, it was billiards or pool. When no phone calls or visitors interrupted the game, he played with surprising intensity, one of his partners discovered. And he was good!

"He was sly and beat me most of the time," confessed Msgr. James Conroy, who served as chaplain for the Victory Noll Sisters and was a columnist for *Our Sunday Visitor*, the national Catholic newspaper based in Huntington. "You couldn't talk to him at all while you were playing; he had no mercy." Msgr. Conroy (then Fr. Conroy) discovered that his billiards partner had a "keen sense of humor. Humorous situations never got by him. But he was the soul of humility. I think he would only do what he was directed to do."

From his vantage point, as a priest outside the Capuchin order, Fr. Conroy observed that Solanus was treated just as all the other friars, despite his reputation. "I don't think the Capuchins were too impressed with him. Solanus didn't seem to stand out to that extent. He was as familiar as an old shoe." Others in Huntington also saw Fr. Solanus in this light. He was clearly a prayerful man, very close to God. Nevertheless, this smiling blue-eyed friar also liked to putter in the garden, loved his Detroit Tigers, and liked to win at billiards, too. He was an approachable holy man.

The young sisters at the Victory Noll novitiate came to see Fr. Solanus in this way, too. Victory Noll superiors wanted their nuns to have some contact with this aging man of God. Because of the limitation of his faculties, however, Fr. Solanus could not serve as any sort of chaplain or confessor at the convent. Instead, in the early 1950s, he was invited regularly to give devotional talks to all the sisters. They would gather in a large hall, with the young postulants seated in front.

Fr. Solanus would almost always talk about the love of God. Often as he spoke, he would become so emotionally moved by his topic that he would stop talking, his eyes would fill, and he would feel the need to pull a large, bright blue handkerchief from his Capuchin habit to dab at his eyes.

To the young nuns sitting right in front of him, the gesture had a Charlie Chaplin sort of flourish. The giggling bubbled up and down the row. But then, the postulants were petrified, thinking of the possible consequences of laughing at such a devout priest. The pause, the handkerchief flourish, the outbreak of chuckling among the postulants, and then the panic were repeated again and again. Solanus would have reassured the young women, had he noticed their discomfort. In his later years, he found more and more joy in young people. And he had always relished contact with children.

In the late 1940s and early 1950s, boxes and boxes of candy began to arrive at St. Felix. They were addressed to Fr. Solanus, but they were sent by friends who knew he loved to give it to visiting children. Though he knew why the candy had been sent, Fr. Solanus did not presume to "claim" it for that purpose. He had spent too many years genuinely vowed to poverty and to obedience. The candy was always handed over to Father Guardian each year, with no suggestion offered as to its use. The guardian had it all shelved in the friary pantry.

When he wanted to have a little candy to give away, Fr. Solanus would quietly approach the guardian and ask for some. It was several years before this little mystery was understood by the house superior. The candy Solanus requested — and carried away by the pocketful — was really intended for his own use and distribution. In June 1950, Fr. Solanus was again hospitalized in nearby Fort Wayne, his legs covered once again with sores and hurting terribly. Two weeks later, the legs were again sufficiently healed to release him. Two-week hospitalizations were very difficult for Fr. Solanus. It wasn't that he was a cranky patient; he was thinking of the stacks of correspondence waiting for him at St. Felix. He also worried just a bit about his gardening enterprises and his beehives.

One of the letters started, but not mailed, before his June illness, was to his sister Margaret and her husband, Frank LeDoux. They had wired about the death of their son Edwin in California. Edwin had apparently been ill for some time. The message Solanus was sending was his predictable blend of sympathy mixed with a spiritual realism about their loss.

> I received your telegram of poor, long-suffering little Edwin. Confident that his was a happy transition rather than a death in the usual sense, I rather congratulate you on having such a chosen one to give to God. . . . Of course I nevertheless sympathize with you on the temporal loss and separation you must for some time expect to experience in this regard.

Somehow, the note of condolence was lost for months. When Solanus rediscovered it only the week before Christmas, he merely continued it and sent it out with a suggestion that "I hope its [sic] better I send it just as it is than start another at this pressing season and as before miss-out [sic] again. . . ." Solanus knew that Margaret and Frank would forgive the weaknesses of a brother who'd marked his eightieth birthday the month before.

After he was "liberated" from the hospital on June 30, Solanus was back at it all. Working with the bees with Fr. Elmer Stoffel, Solanus enjoyed the little creatures he admired so much. According to Fr. Elmer, Fr. Solanus often tried "soothing them by playing the harmonica."

Suddenly, three bees stung Fr. Elmer in quick succession. He fell to the ground, wincing with pain. The assistant bee-keeper, Solanus, stood quietly over him and blessed Fr. Elmer. Immediately, according to Fr. Elmer, the pain of the stings left him and he had no recurrence of swelling or discomfort.

More and more, Fr. Solanus was to be found late at night in the chapel. There, he was happily lost in prayer and even, by some accounts, oblivious to outside stimuli. Benedict Groeschel, then at the novitiate, saw an example of this sort of prayer by Solanus during the summer of 1950.

> It was a very hot night and I was unable to sleep. About three o'clock in the morning I decided to walk around the cloister a few times and came to the side door leading into the friars' chapel. After a few moments kneeling in the dark, I became aware that someone else was in the chapel quite close to me. Slightly startled, I reached over and put on the spotlight which flooded the sanctuary with bright lights. About ten feet in front of me, kneeling on the top step of the altar with his arms extended in an attitude of profound prayer was Fr. Solanus. He appeared to be totally unaware that the lights had gone on, although his eyes were partly opened and he was gazing in the most intense way at the tabernacle on the altar.

Fr. Solanus never moved, at least not that Fr. Groeschel could see. So, after a few minutes, feeling like an intruder in something very private and very holy, the young man switched off the light and left the chapel to Fr. Solanus.

As 1950 drew to a close, Fr. Solanus received an early birthday present that gladdened his heart as no other gift could. On November 1, Pope Pius XII proclaimed the dogma of the

Assumption of the Blessed Virgin Mary. The lifelong devotion Solanus had to the Mother of the Lord seemed to receive a confirmation he found almost too joyous for words. In his heart, he'd always known that Mary was in heaven, body and spirit.

If anything, the coming and going to and from St. Felix Friary increased throughout the early 1950s. More and more visitors came, wanting to talk with Solanus — both individually and in busloads!

But the friars themselves were also traveling more. The postwar economic boom in this Eisenhower era raised the standard of living, making cars more accessible and travel less expensive.

Solanus himself also traveled when he was well. One day, in the parking lot in front of St. Felix, he agreed to a quick driving lesson from a local man. However, the lesson came to a swift and abrupt conclusion

Fr. Solanus chats with a visitor at St. Felix Friary. Even in "retirement," he continued his "front door ministry" of spiritual counseling and healing, begun shortly after his ordination in 1904.

when his sandal caught in the accelerator pedal, giving Solanus and his Huntington "instructor" a few heart-throbbing seconds of concern.

He never learned to drive but always managed to find a ride when he needed one. He still had many friends who provided reason enough to travel back to Detroit. In addition, there were also celebrations, jubilees, and funerals that he wanted to attend. Last but not least, there were certain culinary delights that seemed to be a Detroit attraction for Solanus.

"He would telephone my sister, telling her he was on his way to St. Bonaventure's Monastery in Detroit, having come from Huntington," recalls Fr. Michael Cefai. He was the Detroit pastor at whose parish Solanus had served at weekend Masses from 1938 to 1945. "As simply as a child, he would ask her if he could have some of her spaghetti on the way. He liked a glass of wine. He also liked Maltese cheese cakes." Another trip to Detroit, made in December 1952, had also been preceded by a phone call from Fr. Solanus. He had called his friend Jerry McCarthy, who was, as the St. Felix Friary Chronicle pointed out, "owner of the largest Chevrolet agency in Detroit, and a very great admirer of Fr. Solanus." Father Guardian had decided that the friary's old car, which had 53,000 miles on it, needed to be traded.

Once the decision was made, Fr. Solanus humbly reported his confidence that Jerry McCarthy would give the Capuchins an even trade for a new vehicle! Several days later, Father Guardian, Fr. Solanus, and another friar drove up the St. Felix Friary drive in a 1952 four-door Chevrolet sedan. It was shining proof that the predictions of Fr. Solanus were as reliable as ever.

In August 1952, thirty-seven-year-old Mercedes Ufheil of Huntington went out to see Fr. Solanus with her parents, Mr. and Mrs. Herman Ufheil. The three were concerned about family illnesses and enrolled their family in the Seraphic Mass

Association. Fr. Solanus spoke to them for about one hour, Mercedes reported. He spoke of the healings he had seen occurring over the years through prayer.

"As we got up to leave, Fr. Solanus said, 'Little Mary Ann will be well,' " Mercedes said. Mary Ann was suffering from polio and did begin to improve at this time. But he made no mention of improving health for Wilfred Ufheil Jr. who had suffered a birth injury.

In April 1953, Grace Brady, the sixty-eight-year-old younger sister of Fr. Solanus died in San Francisco following an illness. It was this sister that Solanus, as a young man, was holding when a horse had thrown them both. He had held on to little Grace with one arm and braced his fall with the other hand. In the process, he broke some finger bones which were not properly set later. It was this Grace who had traveled all the way from the West Coast with Owen in 1947 to share in Solanus's golden jubilee celebration as a Capuchin.

It was also about this time that a young black Capuchin brother named Booker Ashe took over as the secretary for Solanus at St. Felix. Like others before him, Br. Booker simply tried to help the eighty-two-year-old Fr. Solanus keep up with his correspondence — usually about a hundred to two hundred letters each day. Around holidays, the name day of Fr. Solanus, or special feasts, the mail would double or triple, he said.

As he always had for other secretaries, Fr. Solanus would draft replies to people with "pathetic" problems, as he called them. Otherwise, according to Br. Booker, there were only a few directions to "tell Mrs. so-and-so that she doesn't have to worry about that. She doesn't have to see the doctor again," etc.

Handling replies was a large job, too, Br. Booker recalled. For a while, he kept a special file of some of those incoming letters from 1953-1956. "I would say that during the time I worked for Fr. Solanus," he said, "there must have been five or six hundred such letters from people helped through his words of encouragement, through his prayers, and so on."

In June 1953, Fr. Solanus traveled to Milwaukee to testify in the beatification cause of Fr. Stephen Eckert. As the summer and autumn months went by, Br. Booker began to fill in as a driver for Fr. Solanus. On longer drives, Solanus invariably talked about "St. Francis in Jesus" and suggested that they say the Rosary or, often, several Rosaries. Apparently, the recitation of the Rosary was something he nearly always suggested while traveling by car. Br. Booker soon noticed that some of the Capuchins teased Fr. Solanus about his love of this devotion.

When Solanus was late for meals, Booker remembered, "one of the Fathers would say, 'For your penance for being late, we will *not* say the Rosary next time we drive in the car.'" Solanus accepted the jest without comment and would often say the Rosary on his own when riding in the car with other friars.

Every friar at St. Felix, however, was very much aware that Fr. Solanus was only devoted to the Blessed Mother because she was the Mother of the Savior he loved so deeply. He was delighted that Pope Pius XII had declared a Marian Year of devotions, opening on December 8, 1953.

In February 1954, Fr. Damasus Wickland, then almost ninety, was anointed by Father Guardian at St. Felix. Damasus had been a classmate of Fr. Solanus, ordained in the same year and with the same faculty limitations. During his last years, Solanus had often gone to visit him during his free moments. Solanus would read the Little Office of the Blessed Virgin to his ailing classmate, who was going blind. On the seventeenth of February, Fr. Damasus died quietly, leaving Solanus as the only living priest ordained with the Capuchin class of 1904. Solanus had hoped that Damasus would live to mark the golden jubilee of their ordination to the priesthood in July.

The men at St. Felix Friary weren't surprised by the tender affection Fr. Solanus showed his dying classmate; this kind of behavior seemed almost routine to them. They had heard so many things about the gifts, the prayers, of Fr. Solanus — and yet, he was a man who lived among them as one of them.

"He was so unassuming that we took everything for granted," explained a Capuchin who'd known Solanus years before in Detroit.

The Capuchins knew the day-to-day Solanus fairly well. They knew and appreciated his holiness. They had less appreciation for his fiddle-playing!

About the time, he also began to "misplace" pies and cakes that devoted local Third Order women constantly bestowed upon him. Solanus would thank the ladies with the greatest sincerity. After they left, however, the aging Solanus, faced with the inevitable stack of correspondence, would push a few books out of the way and shelve the baked goods, meaning to take them to the kitchen later on. But he'd forget! The stale "goodies" would be found later — sometimes weeks later — when a certain book or box of papers was needed off the shelf.

In July 1954, however, the Capuchins began to turn their attention to Fr. Solanus and two other priests in a special way. Fr. Solanus was to get the principal spotlight, as the only man in the order celebrating a golden jubilee of ordination that year.

But he was only too happy to share the focus with Fr. Thomas Aquinas Heidenreich (the Capuchin guardian) and Fr. Cuthbert Gumbinger. They were both silver jubilarians.

The jubilee Mass was held in St. Mary's Church, Huntington, on July 28. Solanus's brother, Msgr. Edward Casey, came to celebrate the occasion. It was a scorching day, but that didn't discourage the crowds that reassembled after Mass in the larger church hall at the town's other parish, SS. Peter and Paul. At the end of dinner and talks, Fr. Solanus concluded with a few short remarks about gratitude to God. Many listening to his remarks had the feeling they'd heard him say the very same words dozens of times before. They probably had! Fr. Solanus had no plans to try to impress with his "sermonizing" anyway. By this

Playing the violin was a favorite form of relaxation for Fr. Solanus. Although he was not a gifted musician, he enjoyed playing such tunes as "Mother McCree," "Pop Goes the Weasel," and "Turkey in the Straw." This picture was taken at St. Felix Friary in Huntington in 1952.

point, his listeners — in and out of the Capuchin order — knew that the real sermon of this priest's life wasn't what he said, but the way he believed and loved.

After the buses left and the Huntington excitement quieted down, Fr. Solanus returned to his daily regimen. As always, it was prayer, letters, phone calls, visitors, community life, outdoor activities, exercise, and then more prayer.

In early November, the St. Felix Friary Chronicle noted, Solanus was slowed down with a cold. But the bed rest was only temporary, and his health and schedule remained stable throughout winter and into the spring of 1955.

One of the calls received one day in 1955 was from a Frank Brady, of Huntington Woods, Michigan. Brady had never met Fr. Solanus but had heard about him. He was calling about his wife, Katherine, who was lying in a hospital bed scheduled for very dangerous surgery. Brady told Fr. Solanus that Kate had suffered whiplash injury to her neck as a youngster, and the condition had developed into degenerative arthritis.

By this point she was in constant pain, but doctors had admitted to Brady that surgery could easily kill his wife and the mother of their four children. As Brady detailed the reasons that the doctors wanted to perform the surgery, Fr. Solanus suddenly interrupted him.

"Oh, no, she won't have the operation," he said. "She'll be out in a few days. She'll be back with those children. Now, tell me, how are the Tigers doing?"

Brady may have been too preoccupied to be able to report on the Detroit Tigers, but he soon reported about his wife's recovery to all their friends.

One nurse he talked to later called Solanus about her own mother. But she received a different sort of response. "Your mother is quite old," Fr. Solanus said gently. "God wants her." The mother of the nurse died two days later, but her daughter was resigned to her loss, seeing it as God's will.

Throughout the remainder of 1955, however, Solanus's own health became more uncertain. He fell victim to colds and flu more often. His legs ached from the varicose vein problem he'd had for many years. And fellow friars could see that his eyesight was failing quickly.

In June 1955, Fr. Clement Neubauer became the newly named guardian at St. Felix. He realized immediately that he would have to watch over the frail Fr. Solanus very carefully. On July 21, the elderly priest's name day, Father Guardian took special note of the contributions he had made as "Director of the Seraphic Mass Association" at the friary.

The chronicle reported thus for that name-day entry, July 21:

Although [almost] 85, Fr. Solanus is still busy as ever, consoling all the people that come to him. Despite the fact that he receives many calls every day, he is a model to all in his faithfulness to religious exercises. His favorite pastime is killing the weeds on the lawn and of course, he is never without his gracious smile.

In November, the friars watched with great interest as their chapel was refurnished and a new altar and platform were put into place. Much of the work was donated by friends of Fr. Solanus, who'd given money for his golden jubilee the year before.

Late in November, a few days before his eighty-fifth birthday, Fr. Solanus learned of the death of his seventy-four-year-old brother, Owen, in Seattle. Owen had been the youngest of

the Casey boys. Several years earlier, Owen had come to celebrate Christmas with Fr. Solanus and the St. Felix Capuchins.
As December neared, Fr. Solanus began to experience much
greater difficulties with his legs.

With St. Felix Friary in Huntington as a backdrop, Fr. Solanus poses for the *Detroit News* photographer in 1956, when he was eighty-five years of age.

CHAPTER ELEVEN

The Doorkeeper Heads Home (1956–1957)

THE FIRST SEVERAL DAYS OF 1956 were exceedingly painful for Fr. Solanus. His skin disease was recurring with a vengeance, and he seemed to find no relief from treatments he'd been receiving through his doctors in Fort Wayne.

On January 2, he coped with the pain long enough to participate in the planning of an amateur entertainment program for the St. Felix community. The friars put on the program the following evening. Solanus, of course, played his violin for his part in it. Nonetheless, his brother Capuchins could now catch glimpses of him wincing with pain when he thought he was unobserved. This was a new development. Before, the friars could only guess at his discomfort.

Erysipelas, also known as St. Anthony's fire, is an acute infectious disease of the skin or mucous membranes caused by a streptococcus and characterized by local inflammation and fever. For years, Fr. Solanus had been combating that and eczema, a skin disease characterized by scaling and itching of the skin. The condition never really left him but was more troublesome for him at various times. The winter of

1955–1956 was one of those periods of more difficulty, and Father Guardian had come to the end of his resources. He had no further ideas about how to help his eighty-five-year-old retired doorkeeper.

After a few phone conversations with Capuchin superiors at St. Bonaventure Friary in Detroit, it was decided to send Fr. Solanus there. Perhaps in the larger metropolitan area of Detroit, a greater range of medical specialists might produce someone who could do more for Fr. Solanus.

"Fr. Solanus left for Detroit today, accompanied by Bro. Gabriel," the St. Felix Friary Chronicle reported on January 12. "Father will undergo an examination at one of the hospitals there."

If the Huntington friary report seemed quiet and understated, the news of his arrival in Detroit was guarded with extraordinary secrecy. The sick man was hospitalized for tests, but all the other Capuchins were asked by the guardian of St. Bonaventure, Fr. Bernard Burke, to say nothing of his presence in the city. Tests indicated that Solanus had some skin cancers on his legs. An operation was scheduled and performed. Doctors then told the Capuchins that Fr. Solanus was in relatively good condition for a man of his age who suffered from the other skin ailments. They admitted that they could not cure the other diseases.

The report on Fr. Solanus was a pretty encouraging one. As if to reinforce his doctors' prognosis, Solanus improved fairly quickly and was released to return to St. Bonaventure. Once in the house, Father Guardian repeated his order to his friars not to discuss the presence of Fr. Solanus in their house. Putting Fr. Solanus under the same obedience, Fr. Bernard ordered him not to accept calls or visitors without permission

— to save his strength. It had already been decided not to send him back to St. Felix for a while.

Solanus gradually improved in this protective environment. His strength returned, and he regained some mobility. Walking no longer made his legs — his "faithful sentinels," as he called them — scream with pain. He began to move around again, but only inside the monastery. As far as the rest of the city was concerned, he was still in Huntington, two hundred miles and a long-distance phone call away.

On February 15, Fr. Solanus received the word that his brother Patrick had died that day in Seattle at the age of eighty-four, news that he took very hard. Pat had been just one-and-a-half years younger than Barney. As boys, they were as close emotionally as they were in age. With Patrick's death so close on the heels of Owen's, Solanus was experiencing the grief of outliving so many of the brothers and sisters he'd loved so dearly. Only three other Caseys besides himself were still living — Edward, Margaret, and Genevieve.

On May 10, with no fanfare or announcement of any kind, Fr. Solanus was transferred permanently to St. Bonaventure from St. Felix Friary. It was clear that

In this *Detroit News* photo, Fr. Solanus is shown reading and meditating on the little office of the Blessed Virgin Mary at the grotto in the St. Bonaventure Friary garden.

Solanus would be a part of the community at St. Bonaventure for the remainder of his life.

Though he began to pick up some of his correspondence load once again, Solanus found himself with more time on his hands. When he was feeling well, he spent his hours in the chapel. If he could not meet with people, he could at least pray for them. And, as he always had, Solanus prayed with an intensity that his Capuchin brothers found remarkable.

Years before, the cleric novitiate and the brothers' novitiate had been separated, and the would-be priests were now living at St. Bonaventure. These young clerical novices couldn't resist occasionally submitting the praying Fr. Solanus to their own "distraction test." Fr. Dan Crosby, who himself was one of those novices, explains:

> On their way to their place in chapel, a novice would deliberately detour to walk directly in front of Fr. Solanus. Other novices would have previously been alerted to the test being conducted. Kneeling in their place(s), they would watch to see if Solanus's eyes would open or at least flutter because of the distraction. To their amazement no change was ever registered. Solanus always passed the test.

Seating was a matter of seniority in religious life, and with almost sixty years of life as a Capuchin, Solanus began to sit at the St. Bonaventure table between Frs. Elmer Stoffel, the master of novices, and Friar Lawrence Merten, the vicar. But if Solanus passed the novices' test with flying colors, the novice master found him less convincing. Some of the novices occasionally came to Solanus for advice, and the master of novices was not happy with what he'd heard of that advice.

So, despite the years spent together in Huntington, and despite the bee sting healing he'd experienced through Solanus, Fr. Elmer distrusted Fr. Solanus. During the suppers for which no spiritual reading was scheduled and conversation was permitted, Fr. Elmer often took Fr. Solanus to task.

"Are you trying to be a saint?" Elmer challenged Solanus, looking at the meager portions Solanus sometimes gave himself. But it was the role the aged doorkeeper was playing with the Seraphic Mass Association that apparently most irritated the master of novices. Over the soup, bread, and vegetables, and with Fr. Lawrence and others listening in, he jokingly told Solanus his own opinions about his "sanctity" and reputation for holiness. Elmer was convinced that Solanus was grandstanding.

"You're trying to work miracles and taking the honor of them while the Seraphic Mass Association is doing the work," Fr. Elmer told Solanus more than once. The tone, according to Fr. Lawrence, was on the lighthearted side, as though one golfer had caught another in trying to fudge on a score.

". . . Fr. Solanus just looked down and continued eating. He would never in any way be grieved or get mad," recalled Fr. Lawrence. "He took it [lying down]. Sometimes he laughed, and other times you could see it hurt a little." But Fr. Elmer was not alone in his view of Fr. Solanus, according to Fr. Lawrence. "Other friars kidded him a lot about many things, even [his] mispronouncing [of] a word. Some would say that he was bluffing the people."

Though it galled some and mystified others, Fr. Solanus unavoidably stood apart from his fellow friars. He tried very hard to draw no special attention to himself. But his unique ministry, which Capuchin superiors had overseen for more than fifty years, had set him apart. The calling had come from a source far beyond the mundane and fallible authority of triennial chapters and elected superiors.

It was a hard calling to leave behind, and Fr. Solanus knew it. After he had been at St. Bonaventure for some months, the word leaked out. He had to go back and forth to doctors, and it was impossible to keep him virtually "incognito" in a city where he was so well known. Before long, people began phoning and ringing the doorbell asking for the aged Capuchin. Screening the requests, Solanus's superiors occasionally said "yes" to visitors. Thirty-minute talks were permitted. When Fr. Solanus was feeling fairly well, Fr. Lawrence would take a few visitors to his room.

Father Guardian's ultimatum about visitors and phone calls grieved Solanus; he obeyed but couldn't really understand the reason for it. As far as fellow Capuchins knew, he expressed that frustration only once — to Br. Ignatius Milne.

"When they were keeping him more confined, he stopped by my desk one day and said: 'Why don't they let me see the people?'" According to Br. Ignatius, the tone and expression seemed to say, "So what if I die in the process? What am I all about?"

But, for as long as they could, the superiors of Fr. Solanus kept the protective prohibition intact. He was not to receive visitors or calls without asking their permission, and then only for a short period of time. Little did they know that their attempts to limit this contact were about to become a lot more difficult.

Late in 1956, the *Detroit News* had talked with the Capuchins about doing a special magazine article about the century of service the Capuchins had given in the United States, Frs. Gregory Haas and John Frey having come to the United States in September 1856 to establish the Capuchin order. The *Detroit News* article was to look at the 100 years of service given throughout the area. The Capuchins thought it would be a good idea.

And then the unforeseen happened.

During the newspaper's advance work for the story, a photographer was preparing to take pictures of some of the novices in choir. Suddenly, he spotted the venerable old priest with the long, white beard — a perfect subject for the photo. The photographer went over to Fr. Solanus Casey and asked him if he would "pretend" to give a blessing to the novices for the photo.

"I will not *pretend* to give a blessing," replied Solanus, indignant. "If you want a blessing, kneel down and I will give one. But I will not *pretend!*" The photographer got the message but also managed to get a photo of Fr. Solanus giving a real blessing. With that picture, the paper essentially made a printed announcement of Solanus's return to Mt. Elliott Avenue.

When the paper finally arrived, the Capuchins were alarmed to see that Fr. Solanus seemed to be a substantial part of the story. The house chronicle at 1780 Mt. Elliott Avenue registered the surprise:

> The Capuchins of Detroit "made the papers" today. Fr. Solanus was spread all over the front cover of the Rotogravure section.

Worse, within the article, Fr. Solanus was the only Capuchin directly quoted. A reporter had apparently asked him his thoughts about his life as a Capuchin. "It's like starting heaven here on earth," Solanus had replied.

For the rest of the day on December 2, Father Guardian and others hoped that the article would not spark an explosion of questions about Fr. Solanus. Among themselves, they thought that perhaps many of the people who knew Solanus had died or lost interest in him. It had, after all, been ten years since Solanus lived in Detroit. But by early morning of Monday, December 3, Fr. Bernard Burke, the Capuchin guardian, could already see that he'd been wrong. Interest in Solanus was anything but cold.

"The Brothers at the front door office desk were suffering a headache from answering the avalanche of phone calls," the chronicle for that date stated. The callers "wanted to know whether Fr. Solanus was available for consultation and blessings." The answer was a polite but firm "no." Those answering the phone explained that Fr. Solanus was very old and had been ill. His health was delicate, they explained, and meeting with visitors would be too taxing. The friends of Fr. Solanus seemed to understand and asked simply to have their best wishes given to him.

Eventually, the rash of phone calls leveled off. The weather turned colder, and Detroiters abandoned themselves to pre-Christmas business. Before the *Detroit News* article, those few allowed to see Solanus had been permitted to do so only with the understanding that they remain silent about it. By Christmas, Fr. Solanus reasoned that, although he was still bound by obedience in accepting visits, he was no longer bound to act like a living secret.

On Christmas evening, young Frater Dan Crosby stopped for a moment in the friary chapel adjacent to the larger church. In a moment, the novice heard a familiar squeaking noise. The young man opened the connecting door to the church just a bit. Fr. Solanus had mounted the steps to the church choir loft. With a few lights behind him, the eighty-six-year-old was in his own world, entertaining the newborn Christ Child. Fr. Solanus was playing Christmas carols on his violin and singing them softly. It was his own Christmas tradition and he'd kept it up for many years.

As the year drew to a close, Solanus continued to enjoy a period of relatively good health. Though he did not talk about it, it must have been an extremely difficult year for him. For the first time since his assignment to Yonkers as a young priest, he was limited in his contact with people, the ones he'd been ordained to serve.

This was a great hardship for Fr. Solanus at the same time that some of the smaller pleasures, the pleasures of life in the

Fr. Solanus takes a moment to pray before a nativity scene. During the Christmas season, he would often play carols on his violin before the crèche in the friary chapel, a tradition he kept up even during his last Christmas, in 1956.

country in Huntington, were also gone. He could no longer take walks in an orchard or tend to bees. The large vegetable gardens, the vineyard, and the lawns of St. Felix were no longer part of his daily walking tour. He had left the country for the city, and even though it was a city he loved, it was painful. Yet Solanus thanked God even for these changes.

In January 1957, however, many of his fellow friars at St. Bonaventure had begun to think that Fr. Solanus was right where he should be. When his superiors checked their records, they could see that he would be marking sixty years in the order on January 14. It seemed right that he should celebrate that occasion in Detroit. He would be able to repeat his vows in the same friary chapel in which he'd said them for the first time.

January fourteenth dawned cold and clear. In the morning, the Capuchins gathered with their jubilarian in the refectory. To forestall the dangers of an overcrowded church, the monastery announced that the occasion would not be open to the public. Nevertheless, a few laymen were already waiting in the larger church when Fr. Solanus and the friars processed into the sanctuary.

There, Solanus stood and listened to the invocation of Fr. Bernard Burke, the guardian. He was only a few feet from the spot where he'd been kneeling when, at the age of twenty-six, he had entered Capuchin life on January 14, 1897.

Finally, he was given a sheet of paper on which was written the vows which he was to repeat. This act formally re-committed him to religious life and to his vows of poverty, chastity, and obedience. But Fr. Solanus had apparently been thinking of his life which, he understood, was almost over. It was really God and his Capuchin superiors who would receive this renewed gift of his life, the life he had left. The thought of it all and of the mercy of God made the deep-set blue eyes fill with tears.

Solanus had to stop reading several times. Everyone in the chapel knew that he had been suffering with more eye trouble in recent years; this time, however, the difficulty was a matter of emotions rather than aging eyes. As he continued to read in his high-pitched voice, his eyes finally overflowed, and he couldn't continue to speak. Fr. Giles Soyka was standing nearby. Giles reached over, gently took the copy of the vows from the hands of Solanus, and finished reading them for him. But Solanus was probably not the only man in the chapel who felt the emotion of the moment welling up inside. Realistically, Fr. Solanus wouldn't have many more occasions to repeat his vows of Capuchin commitment.

In February and March, Fr. Solanus remained relatively healthy. The skin ailments were under control. On St. Patrick's Day, March 17, he wrote cheerfully to his only living brother, Msgr. Edward. He tucked twenty dollars into the letter, telling Ed that the money was for his fund-raising efforts for the missions in the Philippines. During Lent, Solanus continued to get around fairly well and had time to serve in little ways. He was feeling sufficiently mobile one day to serve as "altar boy" for a visiting priest, Fr. Michael Dalton. Fr. Michael hadn't really met the elderly friar who materialized from somewhere in the chapel to serve his Mass. Fr. Michael was nonetheless very impressed when Solanus knelt and kissed the floor in front of the tabernacle as he passed it. This was a gesture St. Francis had urged his Friars Minor to repeat many centuries earlier.

After the Mass, the devout friar — whom Fr. Michael had assumed to be a brother — took him to breakfast and intro-

duced himself as "Fr. Solanus." Something about this elderly
man profoundly touched the visitor, and he asked Solanus to
hear his confession. "I'm only a simplex priest — no faculties
to absolve," Solanus replied to the startled Fr. Dalton. After
Solanus told more about his ministry, Fr. Michael could see
that the faculties God had given to this aged "acolyte" were
really remarkable.

While Fr. Michael unexpectedly discovered Fr. Solanus in
the role of "oldest altar boy," other visitors and callers also had
contact with him in unusual circumstances.

Mrs. Mary Klimczak phoned St. Bonaventure's Monastery
in March. Not really expecting to have the chance to talk with
Fr. Solanus, she asked if she could leave a message for him.
Her overburdened mother was very disturbed emotionally and
at the point of despair. The brother or priest who answered the
phone left for a moment to relay the message.

Suddenly, a high-pitched voice was on the phone — "Fr.
Solanus speaking." Overwhelmed at first, Mrs. Klimczak
regained her composure and began to tell Solanus of her problem.
After asking for a few details, he urged her to read one volume of
The Mystical City of God by Mother Mary Agreda. He also
advised that she try to receive Holy Communion more often.

Mary Klimczak listened very carefully and readily agreed
to it all. As the conversation was drawing to a close, Fr. Solanus
paused, and then assured her, "Things will change today. Come
to see me." Time proved him right.

Not many callers or visitors had this kind of access to the
weakening Fr. Solanus during the early spring. By May, the
skin eruptions that had obliged him to go back to Detroit
forced his return to St. John's Hospital. Capuchin superiors
and Br. Gabriel, a lay brother who had been caring for Fr.

Solanus, were pulled aside, and the doctors confided that the patient might die at any moment.

Fr. Solanus's condition deteriorated dramatically. His physicians did not seem to know how to stem the inflammation. An oxygen tent was ordered to help him breathe. Not long after the tent was in place, however, the patient began to rally. In fact, to the surprise of Br. Gabriel and the medical staff surrounding him, Solanus gained so much strength that he began to sing his favorite Marian hymns!

First, one verse. Then, a second verse through. But when Fr. Solanus sang straight through a third verse and began a fourth, Br. Gabriel could stand it no longer. He was terrified that Solanus might use his last breath just to sing. He begged the priest to stop singing and save his strength. Immediately, Fr. Solanus became very quiet and offered no word of protest. As the days went by, the patient grew a little stronger. Hearing that he was improving, many people found their own ways of having some contact with him.

"How about a blessing, Father?" requested Sister Arthur Ann, a nurse.

"All right," quipped Solanus, "I'll take one!" But he didn't refuse her a blessing or a request she made of him later. Seeing him prepare to say the Rosary in the chapel one day, Sister Arthur Ann impulsively pulled out her own rosary and asked the priest to use hers. She wanted to have it as a keepsake later on, she explained. Reluctantly, he agreed, and laid his own rosary beads in his lap.

When Fr. Solanus felt well enough, he was wheeled down to St. John's chapel. There, he would say Mass or pray his office or the Rosary. He often asked that others read to him there from his favorite devotional work, *The Mystical City of God.*

Somehow, word got around whenever Solanus was making his way to or from chapel. Patients, their families, and hospital staffers would line the hallway, asking him to bless them. He never failed to do so, but he constantly tried to downplay his role as the medium of those blessings.

"I have so often heard people speak of you," commented Sister Arthur Ann one day.

"Yes," he retorted with a laugh, "people often speak of Jesse James, too."

Day by day, throughout late May, Fr. Solanus improved and was finally able to leave the hospital for St. Bonaventure's. However, his days of fair health were very short. On June 14, he was readmitted to St. John's so that his doctors could cope with the resurgence of his disease more aggressively. But he was tiring more readily now and losing weight. Shortly after the second return home, he was rushed to the hospital again. And then again.

The house chronicle at St. Bonaventure recorded the date — July 2. The medical staff at St. John's now discovered that the skin inflammation covered Fr. Solanus's entire body. That made treatment even more difficult. Intravenous feeding tubes inserted to keep him from becoming dehydrated — and even routine examinations — now caused great pain to the patient because of his red, scaling skin.

Doctors were doing their best to make Fr. Solanus as comfortable as possible, but there was little that they could do. From their perspective, this old priest was clearly dying, but he would be dying with great pain.

As the July days came and went, Fr. Solanus lost his appetite and could hardly eat anything. Erysipelas, one of the diseases afflicting him, was known to inflame mucous membranes as well as the skin. Nurses gave him small bits of lemon peel to chew on to slake his thirst.

By this time, Solanus was making no attempt to hide the pain he was suffering. "My whole body hurts, thanks be to God," he admitted. It was very clear to everyone that he was accepting this final and unremitting pain with a Christian joy. Solanus understood very well that he was dying. All of his attention and his mental energy were now focused on salvation — his own and the salvation of others.

Fr. Gerald Walker, the forty-six-year-old Capuchin provincial, came to see him often during these July days. He told him about the many calls, telegrams, and greetings flooding into St. Bonaventure's. The whole city of Detroit was praying for him, the provincial told Solanus.

There was a very special relationship between Solanus and Fr. Gerald, whom Solanus had first met as a small boy. He had come with his parents to see Fr. Solanus during the late 1920s. Over the years, Solanus apparently grew to think of Gerald as a spiritual son, and Gerald revered him as a father. Since Solanus had come back to Detroit, where Fr. Gerald was serving as provincial, the regard and love between them grew even deeper.

"I am offering my sufferings that all might be one," gasped Fr. Solanus, during one visit with Fr. Gerald. "If I could only live to see the conversion of the whole world..."

In recent years, Fr. Solanus — always a keen observer of world events — had become increasingly concerned about that "whole world." He was appalled to see the power that an atheistic nation, Soviet Russia, was gaining. In the previous year, he had been shocked to read about the crushing of organized religion and freedom in Hungary by a nation that denied the existence of God.

He also shook his head often over what he viewed as a growing American materialism. He shared this concern about consumerism one day while talking with Sister Arthur Ann in his hospital room.

"So often people hope to find happiness in money or the things money buys," he told her. "If only they would stop running around, acquiring this or that, instead of seeking happiness only where it can be found — in love of God. They are so foolish." He worried so much about materialism because it jeopardized a sound spirituality.

It was totally in character for him to be so concerned about others, even while he knew he was dying. He simply could not forget about "the people." Serving those people had been his life's work. He seemed to relish and "thank God" for his suffering, in the hope that accepting it would be of service to others.

"I looked on my whole life as giving, and I want to give until there is nothing left of me to give," Solanus confided to Fr. Gerald. Fr. Gerald looked at the emaciated body of the man he'd grown to love so dearly and could barely keep himself from protesting — anyone could see that, at this point, there was very little left of Solanus to give. What he had left to give, however, he was still giving.

Mrs. Gladys Feighan, of Utica, Michigan, was visiting her mother at St. John's Hospital when she overheard that Solanus Casey was also hospitalized there. That was extraordinary good news for her. She had been hoping for several years to ask him to pray for her special intention. When Fr. Solanus was still stationed in Huntington, she'd passed up a chance to take a chartered bus to see him because she'd discovered she was pregnant.

Mrs. Feighan lost that pregnancy, as she had lost two others. She had one living child and longed for another. Because of the Rh factor, doctors advised her that her chances for another baby were very poor indeed. (The Rh factor can bring about *erythroblastosis fetalis*, or Rh disease, which, in certain cases, may result in death for the infant.)

Hoping against hope that she would get a chance to talk with Fr. Solanus for a few moments, Mrs. Feighan went to the nurses' station on the floor where he was. Referred immediately to Br. Gabriel, Mrs. Feighan briefly explained her case. Br. Gabriel left her and went to talk with Fr. Solanus.

In five minutes, she was being ushered in to see the man she'd heard such wonderful stories about. He was extremely thin and obviously in great pain, but his bright blue eyes and a smile were directed entirely at her. To spare him a long history of her troubles, Mrs. Feighan spoke of her great desire to have another child and of the death of three other children through miscarriage.

"A baby!" Fr. Solanus marveled, smiling at her. "For a woman to want a baby — how blessed — and then to hold God's own creation in your hands!" Solanus assured her that her desire was not a selfish one but a very normal one, one oriented to "doing God's work" by bringing up a child as he should be brought up. One didn't always meet women who wanted children, he said. Gladys Feighan then confessed her deepest sorrow — her three unborn children had died without the saving grace of baptism.

"That is not for you to concern yourself about," answered Solanus. "Just have confidence in our dear Lord's infinite love." He continued to talk about God's love and his voice began to tremble with emotion. He blessed his visitor and was quiet for a moment.

"You will have another child, Gladys. You must believe this with all your heart and soul," he told her. "You must believe this so strongly that before your baby is born you will get down on your knees and thank the Blessed Mother. Because once you ask her, and thank her, there's nothing she can do but go to her Son and ask Him to grant your prayer."

There were tears in the blue eyes looking at her so intently, Mrs. Feighan said later. She left, touched by the encounter, pondering the unshakable faith she had seen in the eyes of a holy man who was dying. She began to try to live in that faith from that hour. Five years later, she was doubly blessed with the birth of twins — a son and a daughter.

In the last week of July, Msgr. Edward Casey arrived in Detroit, as did Mrs. Martha Casey, Owen's widow. Both planned to stay at the hospital full time to serve their dying Fr. Solanus. Martha had been the administrator of a nursing home in Seattle, and the hope was that she could help protect Fr. Solanus from visitors still asking to see him.

Family members had been informed by the Capuchins that their brother and uncle was not expected to survive this bout with his illness. He no longer had the strength to fight the disease successfully.

On July 30, Fr. Gerald stopped by to see Fr. Solanus during the evening. He looked weaker than before, Fr. Gerald thought. But Solanus wanted to talk, even though talking obviously tired him, and the provincial tried to slow him down. As Fr. Gerald prepared to leave, Solanus looked at him intently and said: "Tomorrow will be a wonderful day." The meaning was not lost on Fr. Gerald. He walked out of the room and out of the hospital with the words echoing inside his head. Fr. Solanus had predicted the date of his death.

Msgr. Edward had not heard that comment. He rose early on Wednesday, July 31, to say his Mass in the hospital chapel. His special intention was for his ailing brother. Afterward, at about 8:00 A.M., he went to the hospital room to see Fr. Solanus. The patient wanted to talk, and like Fr. Gerald, Edward had trouble keeping him quiet. Solanus spoke of the need for conversion and his longing to evangelize. It was the subject, Edward noted, that always made his brother's eyes glow.

To make sure that Solanus would get a bit of morning rest, Msgr. Ed finally left him. Looking back for a moment, he could see that his brother had a number of covers over him despite the midsummer heat, already beginning to bake the hospital room. Edward turned and went to his own room to write some letters to relatives about the seeming improvement his brother was now showing.

Just before eleven that morning, an orderly, a nurse, and a maid entered the room of Fr. Solanus. They were going to change the bed linens and bathe him. The routine task had to be done so delicately for this patient. His raw and inflamed skin made it excruciating to be moved.

It seemed as if Solanus might be dozing, but then they noticed that he was whispering something they could not understand. The orderly supported his head and shoulders as the nurse pulled his hospital gown over his shoulders in order to bathe him. Suddenly, the blue eyes opened wide and Fr. Solanus stretched out his arms.

"I give my soul to Jesus Christ," he said clearly. The eyes closed and he fell backward a bit, exhaling his last breath. It was just 11:00 A.M.

Just then a couple of the nuns came in, and Mother Aileen had Msgr. Edward phoned. Within a minute's time, Edward came down the hall and entered the room to see that his brother was truly gone. After a minute or two, he began to lead a Rosary for Fr. Solanus but couldn't finish it. Word went out quickly to St. Bonaventure's, and then to Capuchin houses where Fr. Solanus had served or was known. By early evening, thousands in Detroit were in an unprecedented state of mourning.

Back at the monastery later in the afternoon, it was noted that Fr. Solanus had died at exactly the hour he had started his first Mass, on the same day of July fifty-three years earlier. It had been 11:00 A.M. on July 31, 1904, when a dark-haired, bearded young man ascended to the altar in a little church in Appleton, Wisconsin. The life of Fr. Solanus had ended with a mysterious and wonderful repetition.

In Huntington, the friar keeping the chronicle thought for a bit and then made his entry concerning the death:

> We found out about the death of Fr. Solanus, but we are happy for him because he wanted to die and go home to God, where he can now see Him face to face.

CHAPTER TWELVE

A Legacy of Faith and Charity

NEWS OF THE DEATH of Fr. Solanus Casey on July 31 spread quickly throughout Detroit. Friends called and consoled one another. There was the sense among many that they would never again know anyone like him. The evening news in Detroit broadcast the city's loss to thousands more who had still not heard of it. The *Detroit News* and the *Detroit Free Press* were already preparing their obituary notices with follow-up features planned.

No one, however, anticipated the way Detroit would mourn this man many called "Fr. Capuchin."

Soon after his death, the thin, worn body of Fr. Solanus was transported to Van Lerberghe Funeral Home on east Warren Street. The Capuchins were aware that Fr. Casey's following was large. Van Lerberghe's offered ample facilities for a larger wake than could be held at other funeral homes. Visiting hours, it was announced, would begin at 10:00 A.M. on Thursday, August 1.

By 6:30 A.M. that day, crowds of people were already lined up down to the corner in front of Van Lerberghe's. Just before 10 A.M., the funeral director grew concerned about the size

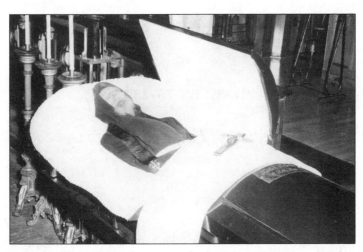

Some 20,000 people paid their last respects to Fr. Solanus, shown here in an open casket prior to his burial in St. Bonaventure Cemetery.

and potentially excitable state of the crowd. Going out to the front, he assured everyone that they would be able to see Fr. Solanus. He then asked them to line up in two columns, so they could pass by the casket on either side.

The people ordered themselves, began to file in, and were soon viewing the man they revered so deeply. Fr. Solanus was dressed in his Capuchin habit, with its hood pulled up over his head. A rosary and copies of the Rule and Constitution of the Order had been laid inside the casket near him. Capuchins were posted nearby to prevent any attempts to obtain "relics" from the habit or body — but also to receive the expressions of sympathy and love for their brother.

The "pilgrimage" continued throughout the day and into the evening. By 10:30 P.M., when funeral home assistants closed the doors, more than 5,000 people had passed by the remains of Fr. Solanus Casey. Among the visitors were people of every age, race, and nationality. Many mothers carried their children by to see Fr. Solanus. Non-Catholics as well as Catholics came.

On the following morning, Friday, August 2, no scheduled visitation was planned. The body of Fr. Solanus was to be taken to St. Bonaventure's Monastery Chapel for further viewing there. However, by 6:30 A.M., hundreds of people were again gathered in front of Van Lerberghe's. They rang the bell and asked admittance until the casket had to be moved. Arthur Van Lerberghe gave his approval, and the people again moved into the viewing room and past the body of the Capuchin they loved.

Shown in this *Detroit News* photo are the numerous priests, brothers, and sisters from many different religious orders who attended the funeral of Fr. Solanus.

The story was the same later in the day at St. Bonaventure's. Hundreds of people stood outside in the August heat in order to get a brief last look at Solanus. By three o'clock that afternoon, 6,000 people had come, stopped for a prayerful moment, and then moved out of the monastery chapel. By Saturday morning, the number of visitors during the wake totaled 20,000.

Many who came stopped to tell the Capuchins that they had experienced healings through Fr. Solanus. Cancer, polio, deafness, psychotic depression — the "litany" of human hurts that had been healed or accepted through Solanus seemed to be as long as the line of viewers. His brother friars listened with growing amazement. "I can see so very clearly now what I failed to see fully at the time," one Capuchin said later. That idea echoed over and over throughout the province and in the friaries where Fr. Solanus had tried to live a low-profile holiness.

At the funeral of Fr. Solanus on Saturday, August 3, his only living brother, Msgr. Edward Casey, was celebrant, while Fr. Gerald Walker, the provincial, gave the homily. Later, Msgr. Edward, speaking to a news reporter, said Solanus "was a very spirited youngster but was also very pious." All the years of his example contributed to religious vocations in the family, he added. Fr. Solanus was survived by two sisters and, of course, Msgr. Edward, as well as by many nieces and nephews, including two priests and twelve nuns. "Fr. Solanus is a family legend as well," commented the younger brother.

But legends have their own proper time for popular recognition. The time for the example of Fr. Solanus to become even better known had not yet arrived. He was buried in the small graveyard on the end of the block that St. Bonaventure Monastery occupied. There were seventeen other friars already there, and the standard gravestone soon indicated that he was not to be singled out from the others:

> Rev. Francis Solanus Casey, O.F.M., Cap. Born Nov. 25, 1870. Ordained July 24, 1904. Died July 31, 1957. Age 86. Religious 60. RIP.

It was only in preparing death cards and the script for the stone that his proper birthday was discovered. For sixty years, Fr. Solanus had not bothered to "correct" the Capuchin record, which had long listed his date of birth as October 25 rather than November 25.

In the months following his death, people continued to come to visit the grave. An enclosure surrounding the grave-

A visitor pays her respects at Fr. Solanus Casey's original burial site. Photograph courtesy of *Michigan Catholic*.

yard admitted anyone who wished to go in. But inside the friary where he had spent so many years, the few articles he left behind were rather quickly distributed or shelved. For a number of years, it looked as though they would remain shelved.

In 1962, seven old notebooks were found among his effects, containing short notes dated from 1924 to 1956 and soon proved to have been the notebooks of Fr. Solanus Casey. They were precious notebooks, filled with the rather small tight handwriting of a man who'd been ordered to keep an "account book" on God's "favors." On careful examination of the notebooks, it was noticed that on six hundred to seven hundred of the entries Fr. Solanus had gone back later to include additional information about healings or the astonishing answers to prayers.

The collecting of other writings and records came later. In 1961, the year before Msgr. Edward Casey died, the last of the Casey sons sat down with author James Derum (*The Porter of Saint Bonaventure*) to share his memories of Fr. Solanus. In 1972, less than twenty years after his death, the accumulated documentation and memories of Solanus Casey prompted the first official step toward further study of his holiness.

The National Council of Catholic Bishops gave a *nihil obstat* (a statement that "nothing hinders" further investigation). A vice-postulator, Fr. Paschal Siler, was appointed to gather information in 1966. Eight years later, he was succeeded by Br. Leo Wollenweber. Br. Leo had known Fr. Solanus, but admitted more recently that "now I know him better than I did when he was living." In 1976, the year of the American bicentennial, the vice-postulator gave a formal petition to Detroit's Cardinal John F. Dearden to initiate the cause of beatification and canonization within the archdiocese.

Throughout the late 1970s and 1980s, the investigation of information, correspondence, and records continued. The official testimony of fifty-three witnesses was taken to Rome from Detroit in October 1984. The "informative process" was conducted by Archbishop Edmund C. Szoka, who succeeded Cardinal Dearden. The testimonies and all other official records were given to the Sacred Congregation for the Causes of Saints.

In general terms, such an investigation looks for proof that the person practiced virtue to a heroic degree. Study of the character of the person's faith, hope, and love of God and of neighbor is mandated as a component in the investigative process. If the Sacred Congregation for the Causes of Saints should vote favorably on the implications of the official testimonies and other documents, the case is passed on to the pope. If the Holy Father declares that the evidence of "heroic virtue" is certain, he declares the person "venerable."

In the later stages of the process, investigators seek proof of miracles linked to the person. If they can substantiate one, the process can proceed to move the cause toward beatification. If the person is beatified, it is accomplished in a public ceremony conducted by the pope. If later study surfaces proof of a miracle occurring after the beatification, the process can move toward canonization.

In July 1987, another step was taken to expedite the investigation of Fr. Solanus Casey's cause. Shortly after sunrise on July 8, Solanus's grave in St. Bonaventure Cemetery was opened. Verification of the identity of the body is a required procedure in the canonization investigation, so workmen raised the casket buried there almost three decades earlier. It was then carried around the corner and into the church, to a room adjoining the chapel.

There, Archbishop Edmund Szoka of Detroit, other Church officials, Capuchin witnesses, two Casey family members, and mortuary authorities gathered to view the body in the room, stifling with July heat. Dr. Gordon Rose, head of the Department of Mortuary Science at Wayne State University, conducted the examination and collected data for a report (to be sent to Rome) on the state of the body.

The report stated that the structural and tissue integrity of Solanus Casey's body was extensive. Msgr. Albert Allen, the archbishop's delegate in the canonization cause, added that the remains were "an intact body — however, not perfectly so." (Some decomposition in both arms had occurred.) The body was then washed, dressed in a fresh habit, and placed into a

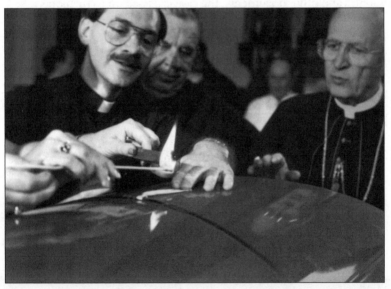

Fr. Ronald Jozwiak affixes the archbishop's seal to Fr. Solanus Casey's casket as Msgr. Albert Allen (directly behind Fr. Jozwiak) and Archbishop Edmund Szoka look on. This *Michigan Catholic* picture was taken during the exhumation and reinterment of Fr. Solanus's body.

new bronze-colored steel casket. The casket was sealed and carried in a quiet procession into the chapel, where visitors could more easily view the grave and pay their respects.

"Fr. Solanus could be the first American-born man canonized," as Br. Leo Wollenweber explained — but no predictions of such eventualities can be, or need to be, made to make the story of Fr. Solanus any more valuable. It was his goodness that makes his story so relevant and inspirational. His was a very selfless love that so successfully communicated an uncomplicated faith in a loving God.

"He had a sparkle in his eyes and a very delightful sense of humor," remembered Mary Casey Molloy, daughter of Solanus's oldest brother, Jim. As a young woman, she had moved to Detroit to work, leaving behind her family in Seattle. During the years she lived and worked in Detroit, the Great Depression swelled the lines of visitors seeking to see Fr. Solanus, and his workload increased. With mixed feelings, Mary would stop in once in a while to see her uncle after work:

I would take my place with other visitors at the Monastery office, sometimes waiting half an hour or more. As he stood up to say good-bye to the person he was speaking with, he might glance up and spot me. Then he would beckon to me to step inside his small inner office. I would feel guilty to thus get ahead of others waiting before me. When he would get a chance to come in and talk to me, he always wanted the news of the family, especially my Dad and Mother. He also asked news of all my Uncles and Aunts in the Casey family. Sometimes if I hadn't stopped in to see him for several weeks, he would call me by phone. In his wispy voice, he would say, "This is your old Uncle just calling to hear how you are and what's the news from Seattle."

Until he headed to his final home, Fr. Solanus Casey never lost his interest and his joy in the news from home, and the "good news" within people growing in faith and thankfulness to the Father of all. *Deo Gratias* — "Thanks be to God."

This is one of the last known photos taken of Fr. Solanus, taken in the spring of 1957.

CHAPTER THIRTEEN

A Man of "Heroic Virtues"

Wʜᴀᴛ ɪs ᴀ sᴀɪɴᴛ?

Trappist Thomas Merton wrote that the true saint wanted to become "a window through which God's mercy shines on the world." For that reason, Merton said, a saint "strives to be holy . . . in order that the goodness of God may never be obscured by any selfish act." Fr. Merton's musings about sainthood had not yet been written when Fr. Solanus Casey, O.F.M. Cap., died on the last day of July in 1957. Without a doubt, however, many who knew Solanus would have asserted that he fit the Trappist's vision of a saint. In his eighty-six years, the unassuming doorkeeper had indeed been a wonderful and ever-open window for God's mercy.

And as the years go by, Fr. Solanus Casey has been increasingly seen in just that light.

On July 11, 1995, at a ceremony in Rome, presided over by Pope John Paul II, Capuchin Franciscans from the United States strained intently to hear each word of a decree being formally read about their own Fr. Solanus.

The decree was short and accompanied by similar decrees for eleven other "servants of God" who had lived over the last several centuries in Spain, Italy, Austria, Nigeria, Poland, and

Germany. Fr. Solanus and the others were said to have lived lives of "heroic virtue." From this day, the title "Venerable" was given to the Europeans, to the African, and to an Irish-American priest whose academic struggles in the seminary had almost barred him from ordination.

For Fr. Solanus and the other eleven "Venerable," this was the first of three major steps toward sainthood in the Roman Catholic Church. As the place that knew him best, the city of Detroit may have cheered the loudest, but Capuchins and Solanus supporters around the world rejoiced. If the cause of Fr. Solanus could progress, he would one day be the first American-born male saint.

But Capuchins closest to the cause in the United States cautioned everyone to be patient and prayerful. Rome alone could canonize Solanus. It was important, they pointed out, to allow the formal investigation still being conducted in Rome to unfold step by careful step.

"Now, we need to wait until the cause is completed, and then, stay in tune for the possibility of canonization when it comes," advised Br. Leo Wollenweber, in the summer of 2006. A patient man, named as the second vice-postulator of the Solanus cause in 1974, Br. Leo had known and lived with Solanus at St. Bonaventure's Monastery in Detroit.

For centuries, that "wait-and-see" caution, along with a thorough and methodical study of Causes, has protected the Church from hasty judgments propelled by personality cults or the runaway bandwagons of enthusiasm. A canonized saint, after all, is a kind of heavenly celebrity, and people naturally gravitate toward celebrities.

But Fr. Solanus Casey was already a celebrity when he died at the age of eighty-six. Thousands of Detroiters attended his wake and funeral. As the 1950s gave way to the turbulent 60s, people from all walks of life and from all over the country remembered him. They couldn't forget the remarkable goodness of the bearded, blue-eyed old Capuchin who always seemed to have time to talk to them.

Some of those supporters joined the Fr. Solanus Guild, formed in 1960, just three years after his death. The founding purpose of the Guild was simply to spread the good word about the life and work of Fr. Solanus. But, it wasn't long at all before the Guild, along with many people from Detroit, were making plans to promote his beatification and canonization. It was almost inevitable.

Those who had come to know him personally or by reputation believed that sainthood for the doorkeeper would be a blessing, a gift for the world.

Catholics, of course, understand that any good and holy person who has died and gone to heaven is really a "saint." A father, a grandmother, a best friend, can all be real saints. That is the first and fundamental meaning of the word.

A canonized saint, on the other hand, is someone remembered and honored around the world and through the centuries. The Church has taught that a canonized saint is undeniably in heaven.

And after careful study and discernment, the Church could claim that this person is a worthy model of Christian virtue and holiness. It is therefore good to imitate a canonized saint. Through that clear, wide window, many more could now get a broader view of God's loving mercy.

In 1966, the Capuchin provincial, Fr. Gerard Hesse, O.F.M. Cap., took the first official step in promoting the Fr. Solanus cause. It had been less than a decade since Solanus's death, but there was no reason to wait. Fr. Hesse gathered reports of twenty-four favors and cures attributed to the intercession of Fr. Solanus and sent them to Rome. On October 4 of that same year, on the feast of St. Francis of Assisi, Fr. Paschal Siler, O.F.M. Cap., began his work as the first Vice Postulator of the cause for beatification and canonization of Fr. Solanus. There was nothing "part-time" about Fr. Paschal's assignment in Detroit.

And throughout Detroit, Huntington, and Yonkers — places where Fr. Solanus was stationed — the stories about his extraordinary spiritual gifts and deeds were finally being recorded on paper. Earlier, they had simply circulated by word of mouth.

Throughout the next several decades and into the twenty-first century, the work of the Solanus cause was the collection of correspondence, personal anecdotes, and reports about him.

Even a handful of the reports showed that the "heroic virtues" of Fr. Solanus were expressed in both ordinary and extraordinary circumstances.

"In the fall of 1936, my brother, Maurice Guerin, was taken ill in Peterborough, Ontario," recalled Canadian Irene Feeley in a written testimony about Fr. Solanus given in 1978. Her brother's diagnosis, she said, was tuberculosis. Within weeks, doctors labeled the disease as "militant", and began to warn the family that he was critically ill. A little later yet, Maurice was said to be close to death. The sanitarium caring for Maurice asked the Guerins which undertaker they preferred.

Living in Windsor, Ontario, Irene was unable to travel with family members to see Maurice for the last time. Instead, late one evening, she called St. Bonaventure's and asked for Fr. Solanus. Once he heard Irene's story, Solanus promised to say

Mass for Maurice the next morning. Irene never forgot that morning. She also went to see Fr. Solanus to talk further about Maurice.

"The Great Doctor above hasn't given Maurice up," he said, smiling and putting his hand gently on her worried head. "Your brother will be all right. He may be in the hospital for a long time — maybe four to five years — but he will be all right when he comes out."

Maurice did make a "miraculous" recovery, Irene claimed in written testimony in 1978. Though he remained in the hospital for three and one-half years, Maurice was healthy enough to later serve for four years in the Canadian Navy during World War II.

There was nothing showy or haughty about the way the Capuchin shared a look into the future with Irene Feeley. She was very sure of that. Solanus had spoken about a coming "miracle" in a matter-of-fact manner. But the priest had humbly deferred any credit for any future healing to the power of God, to the power of the Mass.

In a testimony given in early 1979, Mrs. Rita M. Evison, of Gaylord, Michigan, shared her memories about the generosity and prayerfulness of Fr. Solanus, a man she had never met.

When Mrs. Evison's baby daughter was about six weeks old, in late spring of 1954, Rita noticed that Cynthia was becoming seriously ill. The infant was pale, couldn't digest her milk, quickly lost weight, and was soon diagnosed with a heart ailment.

One night when the baby was two months old, the parents rushed her to the hospital, where doctors said they couldn't control the erratic heartbeat. There was nothing they could do;

the baby, Cynthia, had a heart condition that they believed would kill her.

Back at home after leaving their baby in the hospital, the Evisons tearfully prepared to give their child back to God. But Rita Evison remembered the stories she'd heard about Fr. Solanus, who then lived in Huntington. Grabbing the phone, the frantic mother dialed the operator to get the phone number for St. Felix Friary.

On the other end of the line, a Capuchin brother took the call and promised he'd look for Fr. Solanus. Long minutes passed, and Rita sobbed in grief and desperation as the search continued for Fr. Solanus.

"At first, he could not be located," she testified later. "The telephone operator, who knew I was crying, cut in when the brother said he would look for him. She told me she had heard of Fr. Solanus and said, 'I'm sure he will help you.'"

Finally, as Mrs. Evison recalled, the thin, wispy voice of Fr. Solanus greeted her and asked about her need. Rita explained that the condition of baby Cynthia was desperate. Fr. Solanus replied, "You're going to bring your baby home in a very few days. I'll go down to the chapel now, and I'll pray for her."

The next morning, Rita further testified, a doctor stopped by to examine the dying Evison baby. When he shouted out loud, a nurse ran to his side, thinking the baby had died. Instead, the physician was smiling broadly with the stethoscope dangling around his neck. The baby's heartbeat was back to normal. There were no signs of the irregularity and erratic rhythm that had threatened her life. He had no explanation for the sudden change in a condition which had obviously been congenital.

"It must have been a miracle," he said, shaking his head in joyful amazement. Baby Cynthia did well after that and grew up healthy and strong.

Fr. Ambrose DeGroot, O.F.M. Cap. saw the same generosity, but he also saw the virtue of humility at the very core of the community life that Solanus lived at St. Felix Friary in Huntington. Religious then lived elbow-to-elbow, and Solanus did not set himself apart in any way.

As a newly-ordained priest, the young Fr. Ambrose had certainly heard about the holiness of old Fr. Solanus. "But as I recall," he admitted in a testimony given in 1978, "I was not too impressed. Perhaps we Capuchins do not always recognize heroic sanctity because we live so close to it in our daily lives. And, perhaps, I was a bit jaded."

Fr. Ambrose remembered that Fr. Solanus was then very old and was very slow in many ways. When he told a story or joke, Solanus would "go into all kinds of irrelevant details so that it became boring to listen to him." The story would go on and on until Fr. De Groot — or another young friar — would interject a comment or two to get the old man back on track.

But if Fr. Solanus noted the interruption by someone much younger in religious life, he overlooked or ignored it. "He just never criticized anyone, or said unkind words of anyone," Fr. Ambrose recalled many years later. The gathering of certified testimonies like these began soon after Cardinal John Dearden, Archbishop of the Archdiocese of Detroit, officially initiated the diocesan investigation in 1976. In addition to the testimonies, Cardinal Dearden told the Capuchins that he would officially request copies of all the writings of Fr. Solanus from the dioceses where he had lived. The archdiocese also appointed censors to examine the writings of Fr. Solanus as they were gathered. And so, in the late 1970s, material of all kinds came pouring into a special "Solanus" office in the Detroit chancery. The small, tight, legible script of Fr. Solanus covered many hundreds of pages in a thorough top-to-bottom, economical fashion. "Waste not, want not" was a lesson he had apparently learned well in a family with sixteen children.

Many of the letters of Fr. Solanus — especially those to family members — were long and filled with colorful and warm reminiscences of the past. Written almost always at the end of exhausting fifteen-hour days at his porter's desk near the friary's front door, the letters later provided a good look at the thinking and spirit of the doorkeeper. "Please pray for above poor sinner, Fr. Solanus," he would typically write at the bottom of a photo of himself which he was giving or sending away.

All of the collected Solanus writings were sorted, recorded, and carefully filed for future reference and study by the chancery commission. Included among these primary sources were the seven ledger-style notebooks that Solanus had kept for more than thirty years. These notebooks, as the diocesan investigators discovered, recorded prayer requests made of Solanus and the Seraphic Mass Association. Six thousand "cases," as Fr. Solanus called them, were included in the notebooks.

On 700 of those case notations, he went back later to add some rather astonishing postscripts. Healings were reported; conversions were confirmed; threatened bankruptcies, mental breakdowns, and even divorces appeared mysteriously averted. Great and inspiring stories of astonishing wonders were only hinted at in the terse self-effacing remarks added by the notebook's author.

Even as the process of gathering information about Fr. Solanus proceeded in Detroit, Rome was preparing new guidelines. Bishops around the world had requested that the processes for investigation be simplified. So, in 1983, the Sacred Congregation for the Causes of the Saints released its "New Laws for the Causes of the Saints."

In 1969, Pope Paul VI had already dissolved the Sacred Congregation of Rites, which had dealt with both the causes of saints, and the regulation of "Divine Cult" (prayer and devotional practices). At that time, Pope Paul created the Sacred Congregation for the Causes of the Saints.

Pope John Paul II's writings indicated he also wished to streamline and strengthen the investigation process:

> We also think that the Bishops themselves should be more closely associated with the Holy See in dealing with the causes of saints, in light of the doctrine of the Second Vatican Council on collegiality. . . . It is the competence of the diocesan Bishops or Bishops of the Eastern Rite and others who have the same powers in law . . . to inquire about the life, virtues, martyrdom and reputation of sanctity or martyrdom, alleged miracle, as well as if it be the case, the ancient cult of the Servant of God whose canonization is sought.

When the Capuchins and diocesan officials sat down together to examine the new laws, they found that no dramatic changes in their approach would be needed. In general, the duties of the Bishop or his designated assistants were clearly delineated in the "New Laws":

1. Through the Postulator, the Bishop seeks "accurate information about the life of the Servant of God" and the reasons which support the cause of canonization.

2. The Bishop gathers any published writings of the Servant of God and has them examined by theological censors.

3. If the writings contain nothing against faith and good morals, the Bishop mandates the gathering of all other writings as well as relevant documents for further study and theological assessment.

4. If the cause seems to have merit, the Bishop arranges for the examination of all witnesses proposed by the Postulator.

5. The Bishop ensures that the inquiry into alleged miracles is conducted separately from inquiry into virtues or martyrdom.

6. When all inquiries are complete, the Bishop orders that a transcript and a duplicate copy, together with any books written by the Servant of God, be sent to the Sacred Congregation.

Detroit's Archbishop Edmund Szoka reassessed those six duties of his office in the autumn of 1984. He found that his job in dealing with the Solanus cause was completed for the time being. On October 8, the archbishop officially sealed the boxes containing the testimonies of fifty-three witnesses and other Solanus documents. In all, the boxes held more than 3,600 pages!

Three days later, the Vice Postulator, Br. Leo Wollenweber O.F.M. Cap., Br. Richard Merling, O.F.M. Cap., and a diocesan official traveled to Rome to transport the boxes. The hundreds of pieces of paper represented a claim for one man's virtue. Taken as a whole, the Capuchins believed, they could make a solid, sensitive case for the extraordinary holiness of Solanus Casey.

Almost a decade elapsed before the Congregation for the Causes of the Saints was as certain about the heroic virtue of Solanus as were many Americans. But even in 1995, it seemed that sainthood for Solanus was certainly not guaranteed.

In fact, the cause was entering a critical stage. It is necessary to present proof of one miraculous cure in order to proceed to beatification. Once a person is declared "Blessed," public devotion to the person is then permitted. Churches may be named after the "Blessed" person. Statues or pictures can be displayed. Masses may be said in his or her honor.

For the past several decades, the Vice Postulator's office has studied hundreds of reports of cures allegedly linked to the intercession of Fr. Solanus. In particular, they have focused on cures that took place from 1990 on. And, for the sake of convenience, they hoped to find a viable case among the many that had taken place in Detroit.

"The work now," explained Br. Leo, "is to find a couple of them that have enough documentation and medical records to show that they may have occurred through the intervention of Fr. Solanus, rather than through medical means. Then, if the doctors find that there's not a medical explanation for it, we are directed by the Congregation to proceed with a diocesan investigation in the diocese where it took place."

Later on, if an additional miracle occurring after beatification can be verified, the cause can be moved to the final stage — canonization. Then, at a ceremony in Rome, the Pope could one day declare that the Wisconsin-born Capuchin will be known as "Saint Solanus Casey."

In many ways, admitted Br. Leo, the prospects for that ceremony of canonization for Fr. Solanus do look very sunny. "The Church has seen in recent years that contemporary saints — people from our own times, or own country, and perhaps from our own culture — have greater meaning. In other words, you can relate easier to somebody from your own times and culture."

And, in the wake of recent sex abuse scandals which have rocked the Church, the self-sacrificing example of Fr. Solanus as priest, friend, and advocate becomes increasingly more precious.

"I think we feel that Solanus would be a tremendous role model for priesthood," explained Br. Richard Merling, O.F.M. Cap, Father Solanus Guild Director at the Casey Center in Detroit. "There has been a bigger interest in priests coming to know Fr. Solanus."

Struggling students, added Br. Leo, also might readily identify with a saint who had great difficulty in school. The homeless and hungry might be drawn to a saint who always offered charity, encouragement, and hope with the food he dispensed each week from the Capuchin Soup Kitchen on Mt. Elliott Avenue. No one could be certain about what people in the twenty-first century might think of a man who became a hero because of a life of virtue. But the continuing popularity of Fr. Solanus Casey has astonished Capuchins for more than five decades.

A television profile about Fr. Solanus aired on NBC's show *Unsolved Mysteries* in the autumn of 1994. A repeat broadcast near Christmas, 1994, brought the story of Fr. Solanus into the homes of millions of viewers. At about the same time, EWTN, the Eternal Word Television Network of Mother

Angelica, aired a sixty-minute video about Fr. Solanus, *The Heroic Journey: The Life and Legacy of Solanus Casey.*

After the television coverage, friars at St. Bonaventure's Monastery, where Fr. Solanus lived and is buried, noticed an increase in visitors. From January 1 through June 30, 1995, 15,000 people stopped by to see and pray at his tomb inside the monastery chapel. And when the news circulated that Fr. Solanus was now "Venerable," interest grew even more.

The simple tomb of Fr. Solanus Casey, at the threshold of the public chapel of St. Bonaventure's Monastery, Detroit.

At the monastery Masses celebrated around the anniversary of his death (July 31), the crowds were huge. "It was the biggest turnout that we have had so far," admitted Br. Leo. "We had four Masses and there were over 500 people at each Mass, in a church that normally holds 250. We put up extra chairs all over the place."

The swelling, broad-based, and international interest in the Cause for Fr. Solanus is not a popular movement intended to pressure Rome for canonization. That would be the wrong way to look at the phenomenon, Br. Leo pointed out. He believes it is, instead, a healthy, spontaneous, and hopeful sign from the people.

The Solanus Casey Center Museum contains displays and exhibits connected with Fr. Solanus and the Capuchin Friars.

"The more widely known he is, the more chance there is that his cause is helping people. That's the whole purpose of a cause and of saints. The Church canonizes saints not for their own glory or honor, but so that they might be inspiring examples for people." And each day, in St. Bonaventure's Chapel where Fr. Solanus himself often spent hours in prayer, there appear on his tomb dozens and dozens of tiny white pieces of folded paper. "Before visitors leave, they often add to the snowdrift of tiny slips of paper, each one containing a prayer," reported David Crumm, Religion Writer for the *Detroit Free Press* on July 12, 1995. The snowdrift forms, he said, "daily across the polished oak cover over Fr. Solanus's tomb."

A scribbled petition, a tiny hope committed to paper. During his life, Fr. Solanus understood and responded when people formed long lines to ask for his prayers. Long after his death, many people believe, he is still listening, still interceding in prayer, still pointing out the loving mercy of God.

WORDS AND WISDOM OF FATHER SOLANUS

(From His "Collected Writings")

Appreciation • To know is to appreciate. God Himself can be appreciated — and loved — only inasmuch as He is known.

Atheism • Atheism [is] the very climax of intellectual stupidity, or moral insanity, or diabolically devilish perversity. The height of insanity is not to believe in God, for only a fool says in his heart that there is no God when the heavens and the earth proclaim his glory. Atheism robs man of supernatural hope — the very soul of happiness.

Bitterness • We are never justified in being "bitter" toward anyone except ourselves. Indeed, if we were only one tenth as appreciative as we have every reason to be, our gratitude for what God has done for us — directly and through His creatures, most especially through our immediate superiors — would be such that we would be perfectly content with what we are and what we have.

Burdens of Ministry • Sometimes of course it becomes monotonous and extremely boring, till one is nearly collapsing, but in such cases, it helps to remember that even when Jesus was about to fall the third time, He patiently consoled the women folk and children of his persecutors, making no exceptions.

Christian Life • We are Christians only in as far as we believe in Jesus and keep His word.

Conversion • Only in heaven can we be satisfied as being fully and really converted. Pray for the conversion of sinners — including poor Fr. Solanus.

Crosses • Crosses [are] the best school wherein to learn appreciation for the love of Jesus Crucified.... If we only try to show the dear Lord good will and ask Him for resignation to the crosses He sends or permits to come our way, we may be sure that sooner or later they will turn out to have been just so many blessings in disguise.

Death • Death is the climax of all humiliation, when we must finally give up all and turn all over to God. Death can be very beautiful — like a wedding — if we make it so.

Distractions in Prayer • Do such distractions displease the Good God? For myself, I do not think that they do. I would answer, as I have occasionally done now and then to assure scrupulous souls: No, Jesus is no crank. He knows that we are not angels, but poor sinners.

The Eucharist • How often I regret that daily Holy Communion was not recommended when we were young. I feel now that we missed so much that would have strengthened us against the dangers and temptations of youth.

God's Grace • Were we only to correspond to God's graces, continually being showered down on everyone of us, we would be able to pass from being great sinners one day to [being] great saints the next. We are continually immersed in God's merciful grace like the air that permeates us.

God's Timing • God, who loves tiny beginnings, will know as He always does know, how and when to provide developments.

Gratitude • Gratitude is the first sign of a thinking, rational creature. Be sure, if the enemy of our souls is pleased at anything in us, it is ingratitude of whatever kind. Why? Ingratitude leads to so many breaks with God and our neighbor.

Holiness • As manifested in the lives of the saints, if we strive and use the means God has given us, we too can ascend to great sanctity and to astonishing familiarity with God, even here as pilgrims to the Beatific Vision.

Hope • Hope — the very soul of happiness — [on] this side of heaven.

Human Community • How merciful is the Good God in making us dependent on one another.

Humility • If you can honestly humble yourself, your victory is won.

Justice • Disregard for the claims of justice, under whatever pretext, has always been a manifestation, to say the very least, of shallow thinking, or rather a betrayal of real thinking. Only lovers of justice and truth can possess the Kingdom of Heaven, and to be children of God we must be lovers of justice, truth, and peace.

Living in the Present • Man's greatness lies in being faithful to the present moment. We must be faithful to the present moment or we will frustrate the plan of God for our lives.

Marriage • Marriage should be held as it ought to be, and is, as something sacred, to be prepared for with purity and holiness of heart and embraced in a Christian manner. Those who embrace it should do so determined to bear the burdens of the holy state they enter. They should remember that their duties and privileges are one and the same and must be taken as such if peace is to reign in the individual soul, in the family, and in human society.

Mary, the Blessed Virgin • Mary is our Mother because she has given Jesus wholly to us, human and divine. There is no one else on earth or in heaven that God Himself loves as He loves His ever Virgin Immaculate Mother and wishes her to be known and loved.

Parenthood • God has given a specially beautiful coloring to the love of those whose privilege it is to have become earnest and faithful parents. To raise children for God and society is manifestly pleasing to God. And this, whether by natural generation or adoption (seemingly quite a matter of indifference to Him).

Peace • Peace is the outstanding characteristic of charity. They accompany each other and must begin if really genuine, between God and the individual soul. For the individual, peace is not possible except in the willing service of his Creator.

Penance • God knows as no one else knows how we all and each need penance. God knows we need humiliations whereby we can foster humility. Hence in His love, He never fails to provide occasions for each one to practice penance.

Providence • God's plans are always for the best: always wonderful. But most especially for the patient and the humble who trust in Him are His plans unfathomably holy and sublime. There is a little verse I am sure will profit you to keep in mind and ought to help you foster confidence in God: "God condescends to use our powers, if we don't spoil His plans by ours."

Reason for Life • Life is to live and life is to give and talents to use for good if you choose. Do not pray for easy lives, pray to be stronger. Do not pray for tasks equal to your powers, pray for powers equal to your task. Then the doing of your work shall be no miracle but you shall be a miracle. Every day you shall wonder at yourself, at the richness of life which has come to you by the grace of God.

Religion • The only science that gives purpose to every other science is the science of Religion. Religion is the science of our happy relationship with and our providential dependence on God and on our neighbor. Religion is the science of saving souls.

Resignation • How wonderful the ways of the Good God — when we foster confidence in Him by just leaving at least something that seems important for Him to take care of.

Sacrifices • Sacrifices willingly made for God's sake are always a small sacrifice for the results sure to follow. *Deo Gratias!*

Suffering • We do well to remember how short, after all, it is till our suffering and our time of merit will be over. Let us offer everything therefore to the divine Spouse of souls, that we may accept it as helping Him to save immortal souls, our own included.

Thanking God • Let us thank Him at all times and under whatever circumstances. Thank Him for our creation and our existence, thank Him for everything — for His plans in the past that by our sins and our want of appreciation and patience have so often been frustrated and that He so often found necessary to change. Let us thank Him for all His plans for the future — for trials and humiliations for as well as great joy and consolations; for sickness and whatever death He may deign to plan.

Therefore we should thank Him frequently for, not only the blessings of the past and present, but thank Him ahead of time for whatever He foresees is pleasing to Him that we suffer. We should do this not only in general but in each particular case.

Theological Virtues • Like the Holy Trinity, Faith, Hope, and Charity are one. Theoretically, Faith, like the Eternal Father, comes first, but in both cases they are essentially one.

Tolerance • Be as blind to the faults of your neighbor as possible, trying at least to attribute a good intention to their actions.

Trust in God • In my opinion there is hardly anything else that the enemy of our soul [that is, Satan] dreads more than confidence — humble confidence in God. Confidence in God is the very soul of prayer.

Vocational Happiness • We should be grateful for and love the vocation to which God has called us. This applies to every vocation, because after all, what a privilege it is to serve God even in the least capacity.

Weaknesses • The weaknesses we experience are naturally providential guards against one of the very greatest dangers to holiness — pride.

Work of Humanity • In His divine economy, God has honored His creatures — most especially rational ones — by giving them each according to his ability a part of His own work to do — by participation in His own divine activity.

Worry • Shake off excessive worry and exercise a little confidence in God's providence.... Last year it was something that you now smile about. Tomorrow it's about some thing that will not be serious if you raise your heart to God and thank Him for whatever comes.... How merciful the Good God is, always fitting the back to the burden if not vice-versa, as often is the case!

BIBLIOGRAPHY

The Annals of America, Vol. 16. Chicago: Encyclopaedia Britannica, 1968.

Attwater, Donald. *The Penguin Dictionary of Saints*. Middlesex, England: Penguin, 1965.

Bicknell, Catherine. *Breaking Bread and Mending Spirits*.

———. *St. Bonaventure Monastery, 1883–1983*. Detroit: Fidelity, 1983.

Beard, Charles A., and Mary R. *A Basic History of the United States*. Philadelphia: The Blakiston Co., 1944.

Britt, Albert. *An America That Was*. Barre, Mass.: Barre, 1964.

Capuchin Century Book. Detroit: Capuchin Friars, 1957.

Crosby, Michael H., O.F.M. Cap. *Thank God Ahead of Time: The Life and Spirituality of Solanus Casey*. Chicago: Franciscan Herald Press, 1985.

Derum, James Patrick. *The Porter of Saint Bonaventure*. Detroit: Fidelity, 1968.

Dolan, Jay P. *The American Catholic Experience*. Garden City, N.Y.: Doubleday,1985.

Hyde, Charles K. Detroit: *An Industrial History Guide*. Detroit: S.I.A., 1982.

Longstreet, Stephen. *City on Two Rivers*. New York: Hawthorn Books, 1975.

McDonald, Sister M. Justille, M.A. *History of the Irish in Wisconsin in the Nineteenth Century.* Washington, DC: The Catholic University of America Press, 1954.

Mead, Howard, Jill Dean, and Susan Smith. *Portrait of the Past: A Photographic Journey Through Wisconsin.* Madison, WI: Wisconsin Tales and Trails, 1971.

O'Grady, Joseph P. *How the Irish Became Americans.* Boston: Twayne Publishers, Div. of G.K. Hall & Co., 1973.

Patterson, Jerry E. *The City of New York.* New York: Harry N. Abrams, 1978.

The Private Side of American History, Vol. II, edited by Thomas R. Frazier. New York: Harcourt Brace Jovanovich, 1975.

Sowell, Thomas. *Ethnic America.* New York: Basic Books, 1981.

The Solanus Casey Center, Detroit, is a Capuchin ministry that "strives to be a place of pilgrimage, healing, reconciliation, and peace." Pictured here is the Center entrance, as approached through the Creation Garden.

NOTES

Fr. Benedict J. Groeschel,
~ C.F.R. ~

Questions and
Answers
About Your
Journey to God

OurSundayVisitor

Bringing Your Catholic Faith to Life

www.osv.com

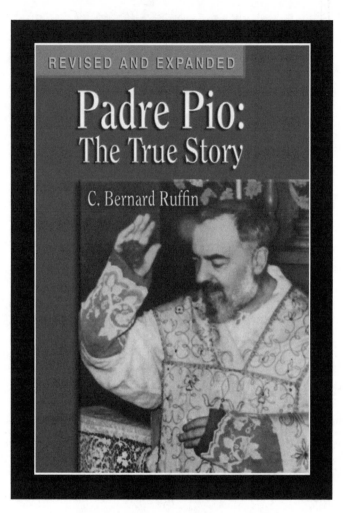

REVISED AND EXPANDED

Padre Pio:
The True Story

C. Bernard Ruffin

Our Sunday Visitor

Bringing Your Catholic Faith to Life

www.osv.com